Medieval Days and Ways

By Gertrude Hartman

THE WORLD WE LIVE IN: AND HOW
IT CAME TO BE

THESE UNITED STATES: AND HOW
THEY CAME TO BE

MEDIEVAL DAYS AND WAYS

Medieval
days and ways

By
Gertrude Hartman

The Macmillan Company
NEW YORK
1960

TO

Q. F. C.

AND

L. B. M.

Foreword

ℱoreword

The Living Past

THIS book tells how people lived in Europe during the
Middle Ages. You will see knights and ladies in the halls
of the castles, or riding out to hunt and to hawk, or engaging
in their tournaments; you will see the poor peasants toiling
in the fields of the manors and the craftsmen at work in their
little shops in the towns; you will see the people of the towns
building their cathedrals and the monks in the monasteries
making their illuminated books. And, whenever possible,
the people of the day tell about their life in their own words.
In the quaint language of the time, old chroniclers describe
many stirring events, troubadours recite their romances for
you, and the mummers and the guildsmen give their plays.

Through reading history we are able to link our life with
that of the people who lived in the world before us. In the
building up of civilization every generation of people has
contributed its share. In the early days of the world, when
men first came upon the earth, all the land was a vast wilderness, and man lived a life but little different from that of the
animals that shared the earth with him. But age after age
man struggled to improve his way of living, each generation
adding something to what had been accomplished before it,
and creating something which endured after it and became
the foundation upon which the next generation built. It is in

this way that almost everything we have in the world today has been gradually developed through past ages.

If we want to understand the world we are living in we must see how, through the ages, it came to be as it now is. We must know how people lived in the past, what they thought, what they believed, what they did day by day, what they learned about nature's ways, and what improvements in life they brought about.

In reading about the Middle Ages you will discover how many contributions the people of that great period made to civilization, and you will see how their descendants, who settled this country, brought here with them many of the customs and ways of living they had known in their old-world homes and passed on to us all that their ancestors in Europe had learned.

Contents

Foreword

The Dark Ages

In Castle Days

The Medieval Church

ix

Towns and Town Life

From Medieval to Modern Times

Conclusion

x

The Dark Ages

Rome and the Barbarians

FOR centuries mighty Rome ruled the ancient world. Nation after nation she conquered, and at the height of her power her far-flung empire embraced western Asia and northern Africa and in Europe included all the land west of the Rhine and south of the Danube River.

North of the Roman Empire in Europe stretched a vast region of forests, extending all the way from the Danube River to the North Sea. In this wild country, beyond the farthest limits of the civilization of the day, lived many barbarous tribes of people. Among them were the Goths, the Vandals, the Burgundians, the Lombards, the Franks, and the Angles and Saxons, who lived farther north. Still farther north dwelt the Norsemen.

These people who lived north of the Roman world were very different from the Romans. They were tall, with flaxen hair and blue eyes. Their clothing was usually the skins of animals, or coarsely woven woolen cloth, thrown about them, with the arms and shoulders left bare. Their houses were rude huts of roughly hewn timber, often grouped together in a clearing in the forest to form a straggling village. A group of neighboring villages formed a tribe. The people

13

of each tribe selected their strongest and bravest warrior as their chief.

These Germanic tribes were fierce fighters, and the Romans, who had conquered so many nations, were never able to conquer these barbarians. They had to content themselves with keeping them out of the empire by strong fortifications along the Rhine and Danube rivers.

For nearly five hundred years Rome kept her frontiers safe against the northern barbarians. But Rome, which had been so strong in earlier days, in time grew weaker and weaker, and toward the end of the fourth century the tribes of the north began to burst through the Roman barriers. The first were the Goths, who lived just north of the Danube River. A horde of fierce, warlike people from the wilds of Asia, called the Huns, swept like a whirlwind over Europe, plundering and destroying everything in their way. When the Goths heard of their approach, they looked across the Danube at the well-guarded land of the Romans and sent an imploring message to the Roman emperor asking him to allow them to cross the river and come under the protection of Rome. The emperor granted their request, and thousands of Goths, with their wives and children and their herds and cattle, crossed the Danube and settled down. But the Romans ill-treated the Goths, so that they rebelled and decided to form a kingdom of their own in Roman territory.

Other tribes of barbarians broke through the frontiers and wandered southward and westward within the Roman Empire in search of new lands and new homes. For years the Romans fought to defend their empire against these invaders, but at last came the time when they could no longer do so. One bit of land after another was split off from the old empire, and in the year 476 the Roman emperor was driven from his throne and the Roman Empire ceased to exist in Europe. Hundreds of little independent kingdoms were being formed in the lands once ruled by Rome.

In 418 a tribe of Goths burst into Spain and founded a kingdom there. For nearly three hundred years they held this land against all enemies. Then in 711 they were utterly defeated by an army of Arabs—or Moors, as they were sometimes called. The Moors were followers of a religious leader named Mohammed, who lived in Arabia.

In early life Mohammed was a humble shepherd in Arabia, and later he became a camel driver, conducting caravans across the desert. As he traveled back and forth with his trains of camels, he spent many a solitary night on the desert, gazing up at the starry sky. At length he began to see visions in which an angel appeared to him with messages from God. Mohammed became convinced that it was his duty to reveal these to mankind.

At first few people would listen to Mohammed, and he and his handful of followers were driven out of his own city of Mecca. Another town, Medina, received Mohammed, and many of the people there were converted to his belief. At length Mohammed was strong enough to return to Mecca and capture it. From that time on, the new religion spread rapidly, so that before the prophet died most of the people of Arabia were Mohammedans.

Before the time of Mohammed the Arabs had played no

15

great part in the world's history, but for a century after Mohammed the caliphs, as the rulers who followed the prophet were called, became ambitious for more lands. Inside of seventy years they had conquered a vast empire in Asia and had spread all over northern Africa.

In 711 the Arabs planned the subjugation of France, Germany, and Italy. They crossed the Strait of Gibraltar, advanced north in Spain, and established a kingdom there which extended to the Pyrenees Mountains.

The Arabs were the most cultured people of the time. During the tenth century, which was so dark a period in the rest of Europe, Spain under the Moors became the most civilized country in Europe. They built beautiful churches —or mosques, as they were called by the Mohammedans— and beautiful palaces. Of these the mosque at Cordova and the palace of the Alhambra, at Granada, are still standing.

One of the tribes that invaded the Roman Empire was known as the Franks. They crossed the Rhine River and settled in Gaul. At first they were divided into many little tribes, each ruled over by its own king, but little by little these people were united into one nation, known as France, the kingdom of the Franks.

The Moors who had conquered Spain, wishing more land, crossed the Pyrenees Mountains to conquer the kingdom of the Franks. For a time it looked as if the Moors might be masters of all Europe. But an able leader by the name of Charles Martel met the invaders at Tours in central France with a host of fighting men from all over the Frankish lands. In a fierce struggle the Moors were driven back into Spain

16

Charlemagne. (From a painting by Albrecht Dürer.)

never to return. Thus Europe was saved from falling into the hands of the Arabs.

In time the kingdom of the Franks became one of the most prosperous and civilized parts of Europe. Their most famous king was Charlemagne, who was crowned king in 768 and ruled the Franks for almost half a century. On every border warlike peoples were constantly threatening his lands. Charlemagne not only defended his own country but conquered new lands. His conquests gave the Franks a larger empire than had existed since the old Roman Empire broke to pieces and made him the greatest ruler in Europe. Charlemagne made good laws for his kingdom. He did all he could to encourage learning and make his people more civilized.

After the death of Charlemagne it proved impossible to hold his vast empire together. The later rulers of Frankland were not strong men like their ancestor. By the middle of the ninth century his kingdom was broken up. East Frankland became Germany, West Frankland became France, and another part became Italy. Each country had its own king and developed in its own way as an independent kingdom.

England, or Britain, as it was called in the early days, was a Roman province and was ruled over by Rome for almost four hundred years. When the tribes were overrunning the Roman Empire the Roman legions, which had been stationed in Britain, were recalled to help defend Rome, and the Britons were left undefended. Terrible times followed. The fierce Picts and Scots, tribes that dwelt to the

18

north of the Britons, began to make raids into Britain, and the Britons were not strong enough to repel them.

At that time roving bands of Angles and Saxons, tribes from the northwestern coast of Europe, across the North Sea, began coming to the shores of Britain, and the Britons asked these sea rovers to help them against their enemies. The Angles and Saxons repelled the Picts and the Scots, but when they discovered what a good land Britain was they proceeded to conquer it for themselves. The Britons were driven westward into the mountainous districts of Wales and Cornwall, where they were more protected; their country was divided up into a number of little kingdoms, which were finally joined together under the rule of one king; and Britain came to be called Angle-land—or, later, England.

Three or four hundred years after the Angles and Saxons settled in England, the Danes, a new race of sea rovers, came swarming upon its coasts. Though the Danes came at first to plunder, they were on the lookout for new homes and soon began to stay in England. A brave and able king of the Anglo-Saxons, known to history as Alfred the Great, stopped their conquests. King Alfred was a wise and good king. He made many improvements in his kingdom. He was interested in giving his people good laws, and he punished evildoers severely.

From very early times there dwelt in the far north of Europe, in the countries we now call Norway, Sweden, and Denmark, a hardy race of people called Norsemen, men of the north, or Vikings—which means men of the creeks and bays, because their coast was indented by many long narrow inlets. The character of their native land made these people natural seamen. Inland their country was so wild and rugged that most of the people dwelt along the coast. They raised what crops they could; but the soil was so rocky and barren that they had to depend largely on fish for their food, and they spent most of their time on the sea. The dense northern forests supplied plenty of wood for ships, and in the course of time the Norsemen learned to build seagoing ships and became skilled and daring sailors. The ships of these hardy sailors were long and narrow, with forty to fifty oars and a large square sail. The prows were high and were carved to look like huge dragons' heads, and the sterns like their tails. All around the sides of the ships hung the wooden shields of the warriors.

The Norse had taken no part in the earlier invasions of Europe, but in the ninth century they began exploring the

Ships of William of Normandy crossing the English Channel. (From the Bayeux Tapestry.)

northern sea in every direction in their long, many-oared dragon ships. Some sailed to Iceland, Greenland, and Labrador, and it is thought that some even reached the coast of this country. They learned about the beautiful lands to the south of them, and under a leader, named Hrolf—or Rollo—a band of them made their appearance on the northern coast of France and forced the king to grant them a stretch of land lying along the English Channel. Rollo divided up this land among his followers.

As time passed, the Northmen—or Normans, as they came to be called—gave up their old heathen customs and adopted the language and manners and customs of the Frankish people among whom they had settled. Thus, in time, the descendants of Hrolf became the polished and rich dukes of Normandy and developed a fine civilization in northern France.

In 1066 William, duke of Normandy, decided to attack England. He assembled a large fleet, sailed across the

A scene from the Battle of Hastings. (From the Bayeux Tapestry.)

21

English Channel, and fought the English forces under King Harold at Hastings in the south of England. Harold was defeated, and the English army was cut to pieces. After this battle William took possession of England and was accepted by the people as their king. He is known to history as William the Conqueror.

To the Norman knights who helped him win England William gave rich lands, and they became the ruling class in the country. The Normans spoke differently, dressed differently, and lived differently from the English, and they carried into England their customs and language. At first they looked down upon the Anglo-Saxons for their ignorance and their rude ways, but gradually both races were united into a strong nation.

We have seen how the invading tribes of barbarians migrated into the lands formerly ruled over by Rome. For four hundred years the old Roman world was the scene of violence and destruction. Roman towns were plundered and priceless treasures destroyed. Art, literature, and learning declined, and it seemed as if the marvelous civilization of the ancient world was being entirely swept away. Historians have called this period, when the uncivilized tribes were overrunning Europe, the Dark Ages.

But In time the migrating tribes settled down and established kingdoms in various parts of Europe under their chieftains. These little warring kingdoms were united by strong chiefs into larger kingdoms and thus new nations— France, Spain, Italy, England, and so on, gradually were formed by the descendants of the people who had invaded the Roman Empire. Some of the tribes of barbarians had remained in northern Europe, and these also developed into nations—Germany, Denmark, Norway, and Sweden.

All these people gradually learned the ways of civilization, and Europe entered upon a new period of history, the Middle Ages. Although the people of Europe were divided into various nations their ways of living were similar. How they lived in the thousand years following the fall of Rome we shall tell in this book.

In Castle Days

I

Lords and Vassals

DURING the centuries when the different tribes were conquering and settling various parts of Europe there were no regular governments. There was no law and no means of keeping order. The king claimed all the land in his kingdom and kept large parts of it for himself; the rest of it he divided among the followers who had fought with him to get it, on condition that they would help him defend the land in case of attack. These men, having more land than they could defend, divided up their land among other men, who in turn promised to be loyal to them and aid them in time of war.

The chief business of the feudal lords was fighting to get land and then fighting to keep the land they had fought to get. Every strong man took the land he wanted and held it until someone stronger took it away from him. For hundreds of years all Europe was given over to fighting and plundering.

In a time of such constant danger the most important thing in the world to everyone was safety. Weaker men were therefore willing to attach themselves to some more power-

27

ful leader for the protection he was able to give and to agree to serve him and be faithful to him. The powerful men needed men to help them fight their battles, and thus they secured military followers. Every man owed service to someone higher up.

The weaker man was called a vassal, and the stronger man was called an overlord. When a man wished to become the vassal of another he went down on his knees before him, bareheaded and unarmed, and took a solemn oath to be his "man"—that is, he promised to serve him faithfully and to fight for him when necessary in some such words as these: "For each and all of these lands I make homage and fealty with hands and mouth to thee, my lord, and I will defend thee, my lord, and thy land against all invaders, so help me God and the saints." This was called the oath of fealty. Then the lord would raise his future vassal to his feet and would present him with some little object, like a twig of a tree, or a clod of earth, as the symbol of the land he was giving him. This ceremony was called "doing homage."

This organization of society for protection is known as the feudal system. It was useful in a time of disorder and danger and soon spread all over Europe.

The constant warfare of the feudal age made it necessary for people to live in massive stone structures like fortresses, surrounded by high walls and defended by many men-at-arms. The high top of the surrounding wall of the castle was made broad and flat, so that warriors could stand there and fight; and on the outer edge of it a thinner wall, called

The Castle of Coucy on a hill in northern France, built in the
thirteenth century. (A restoration by Viollet-le-Duc.)

a parapet, was raised a little higher than a man's head to protect the soldiers. Every few feet on this raised edge there were narrow openings through which skilled archers and crossbow men could shoot arrows, or hurl stones, or pour burning pitch down on their foes below. High towers were built at every corner of the wall, which overlooked the country for miles in every direction, and there sentinels were always on guard to sound the alarm at the approach of an enemy.

Castles were usually built high up on some rocky cliff, or on a faraway island, hard to reach, or on a steep headland jutting far out into a river or lake. When a castle was not in some place like this, where it was protected by some natural defense, it was surrounded by a wide, deep ditch, called a moat. This was always kept filled with water and could be crossed only by a drawbridge, which could be drawn up at a moment's notice, leaving no way for enemies to get across the moat. The doorway of the castle was of solid oak, several inches thick, bolted by heavy iron bars. Behind it was a strong iron grating, called a portcullis, which could be dropped down in an instant. The chief porter, who had charge of the door, lived in a turret above the entrance to the castle and kept a keen eye on all who approached, for it was his responsibility to see that only friends and friendly travelers entered the castle and to lower the drawbridge only for those who were welcome. Medieval Europe was covered with thousands of these strongholds.

When an attack was made upon a castle the best way to get to the top of the high wall surrounding it was to use a

Attacking a castle.

movable tower. This was a wooden shed, several stories high, set on rollers. The moat was first filled with turf and the trunks of trees to make a roadway across it. Then the great tower was rolled up to the wall, a drawbridge was dropped from its upper story to the top of the wall, and over this

A battering ram.

swarmed the besiegers. The defenders threw burning pitch at the tower in the hope of setting it ablaze, but it had been carefully covered with the skins of animals to prevent it from being set on fire.

Another device used by those attacking a castle was a battering ram for making a hole in the stone wall. It was a heavy beam of wood with a ram's head at the end. Men ran with it up to the wall, beating again and again at the same spot, trying to make a breach in the wall through which the besiegers could get into the castle yard. There were also catapults for hurling stones or bolts of red-hot iron over the walls. A trigger was pulled, which sent the missile sailing up with great force over the wall. There were scaling ladders, too, which soldiers set up against the wall. Sometimes the besiegers dug their way under the wall and surprised the inhabitants of the castle by entering in the middle of the night.

If those attacking a castle were not successful in scaling the walls, or battering them down, or undermining them, they often adopted the slower method of a siege and tried to starve the inhabitants by cutting off their supplies; but the storerooms of every castle were stocked with provisions enough to last at least for six months.

When a noble and his vassals and men-at-arms sallied forth to attack the castle of some rival, or to raid an enemy's lands, they protected their bodies with steel armor so strong that scarcely any weapon could pierce it. The earliest armor was made of leather, or cloth, thickly padded and quilted. But this was not strong enough for protection, so interlaced rings of metal were sewed in rows on this tunic. Later came chain mail of strong, interlaced rings of steel worn over quilted or leather garments, with a hood of the same for the head. The next improvement was to fasten

33

plates of steel at certain places like the elbow or the knee. Little by little chain armor disappeared entirely and whole suits of armor made of overlapping steel plates took its place. The head of the warrior was protected by a steel helmet with a visor that could be pulled down over the face, in which the only openings were small slits to see and breathe through. His chief weapons were a lance and a sword.

Medieval warriors fought on horseback. It would have been impossible for them to fight on foot. It took a powerful horse to carry a knight in his armor. And the horse had to be well protected by armor, because if a horse was killed, or wounded, a knight, encased in his heavy armor, was helpless.

When the closed helmet came into use, entirely covering the face of a knight, the custom arose of emblazoning some distinctive mark, or device, on his shield or breastplate by which he might be distinguished in battle. This device was called his coat of arms. Each knight chose a device which

belonged to him alone, and it became hereditary in his family. All sorts of strange fantastic creatures—griffins, dragons, and unicorns—came to be used. Frequently a device was chosen which had some connection with an important event in the wearer's life, or one suggested by his name.

At first every individual consulted his own fancy in choosing his device, but as time passed this resulted in much confusion, so a central authority became necessary to register devices and to make rules. The officers upon whom this duty fell were called heralds, and the subject of their jurisdiction came to be known as heraldry.

II

Behind the Battlements

INSIDE the outer protecting wall of the castle were a number of buildings, for a castle had to house many people. There were the stables for the horses, rough quarters for the grooms and hostlers, and barracks for the men-at-arms. There, also, were the shops of the armorers, the smith, the carpenter, and other workmen, and the little chapel where the lord and his family attended daily mass. Beyond the first courtyard was another stone wall protecting the inner courtyard and buildings.

The most important room in the castle was the hall, for it was the common meeting room of the household. It was a large rectangular room, lofty and spacious. The walls were of paneled wood or of gray stone, unplastered and rough. The floor, too, was flagged with great stones. Instead of a ceiling there were usually rafters of solid oak, often richly carved and ornamented in color. The windows of the finest halls were filled with beautiful stained glass, but in the dwellings of the less wealthy the glass was coarse and greenish and made in small round pieces, for glass in those days was too rare and expensive for ordinary use. At the end of the room was a big stone hearth where huge logs could be

36

piled, to burn with cheerful blaze and warm the people during the long cold winter months.

In the early centuries carpets and rugs were rare. The floors were usually covered with rushes, which were fragrant and pleasant while they were fresh, but which in time often became dry and dirty. Shields and clusters of lances were hung on the walls. Other spaces were adorned with antlers and the heads of wild boar, while from the beams of the roof hung gay banners emblazoned with the coat of arms of the lord of the castle. In the fourteenth century the bare stone walls were often covered with tapestry, rich in color and design, on which were woven various scenes from history or a favorite romance of the times. These hangings brought warmth and beauty into the halls.

During the earlier centuries of the Middle Ages the hall served as living, dining, and sleeping place for everyone, with recesses used as retiring places by the family. But as people became more civilized the halls came to be used only for public functions, while the family of the lord lived in a more private apartment adjoining it.

A medieval bedroom lacked many of our modern conveniences, but it was beautiful. The floor was inlaid with checkered tiles, and the leaded windows were gay with heraldic glass. There was usually not much furniture in it —one or two chairs, with high carved back and arms; a small table; a footstool covered with silk; an oaken cupboard. The most striking piece of furniture was the bed. It was a stately four-poster, set in an alcove and canopied with beautiful curtains of damask or brocade, which could be drawn around to inclose it entirely, to keep out drafts. At the foot of the bed was a huge chest richly ornamented and carved with the emblem of the owner, in which clothes were kept. On the wall near one of the windows was a large crucifix of carved wood. Before it the lord and lady knelt on

A medieval apartment. (A restoration by Viollet-le-Duc.)

red silk cushions each night and morning to say their prayers.

In the lady's bower the lord's wife, with her handmaidens and numerous serving-women, spent most of her time directing the spinning, weaving, embroidering and sewing, caring for her children, and managing the daily work of her big

38

Medieval ladies carding, spinning, and weaving.

household. In addition she had her social duties, the most important of which were acting as a gracious hostess to guests, nursing wounded knights, and training pages in the ways of chivalry. A girl of the Middle Ages was taught the things a medieval lady was supposed to know. She learned to sing and to play accompaniments on some musical instrument. She must ride well. She must be skilled in needlework. She must know how to be beautiful at tournaments and other ceremonial occasions.

It was in the hall that the whole household gathered at mealtimes. Across one end of it was a platform—or dais—raised a step or two above the main floor, on which a high table was placed. In the center of the side near the wall was the seat for the lord, sometimes raised on a throne or an especially built high chair. His family and most honored guests were placed on each side of him, facing the rest of the company. No one was placed on the opposite side of the table. It was left entirely open so that the lord and his guests might see and be seen by the rest of the company. The other tables, long and narrow, were arranged down the whole length of the hall at right angles to the lord's table, with long benches along each side.

At one end of the hall was a passageway leading to the kitchen. Sometimes this was a near-by building separate from the hall. It was a large vaulted room, perhaps a hundred feet long, the headquarters for the servants, where a great deal of work had to be carried on. It had big ovens for baking and huge open fireplaces, where whole deer or sheep could be hung on spits and turned before the fire.

Immense copper cauldrons hung over the fireplaces. There were large tables with solid oak tops, and on the walls hung many utensils—ladles, strainers, graters, saucepans, and so on.

Preparing the meals for a big house, with its many inmates and guests, was no easy matter, and the chief cook was a very

A fourteenth-century cook. (From the Luttrell *Psalter.*)

important member of the household. His responsibilities were many. He had to provide all kinds of elaborate dishes and fancy table decorations. He must know how to make many complicated soups, stews, sauces, and desserts. He ruled over dozens of lesser cooks and scullions, for the richer households had from fifty to a hundred servants to cook and clean. As a mark of his office, he carried a large wooden

41

spoon, which he used for testing the soups and other dishes and also for chastising those who failed to obey his orders.

Dinner at a rich nobleman's house might include as many as ten or twelve courses, mostly meat, game, and fish, finished off with a quantity of rich pastries and sweetmeats. When it was in preparation the kitchen presented a busy scene and

Roasting fowls and a rabbit before a fire. (From the Luttrell *Psalter.*)

was fragrant with appetizing odors, as the cooks and bakers employed all their art in preparing a variety of fancy dishes, and scullions ran about turning the meats on the spits or blowing up the fires with bellows.

Nearly every dish was soft and mushy. Everything was mashed or cut into very small pieces, and all dishes were so smothered in spices that it was almost impossible to tell what they were originally made of. Today we can scarcely appreciate the fondness of the medieval people for spices. Not only meat, but cake, bread, and wine were spiced. Every large household kept a store of spices, which were

42

very expensive, and the "spicery" was superintended by a person whose duty it was to give out the proper quantities of these choice ingredients to the cooks.

Pastries made of chickens, grouse, pigeons, and other meats were often elaborate masterpieces of the cook's art. Here is the recipe for one taken from a medieval cookbook:

Preparing dinner. (From the Luttrell *Psalter*.)

Take a pheasant, a hare, a capon, two partridges, two pigeons and two conies; chop them up, take out as many bones as you can, and add the livers and meats, two kidneys of sheep, force meat made into balls with eggs, pickled mushrooms, salt, pepper, spice, vinegar. Boil the bones in a pot to make a good broth; put the meat into a crust of good paste, made craftily into the likeness of a bird's body; pour in the broth, close it up and bake well. Serve it with the

43

head of one of the birds at one end, and a tail at the other, and divers of his long feathers set cunningly all about him.

Sometimes a cook would surprise his lord by making a huge pie full of little live birds, which fluttered out and flew high up in the air when the crust was cut open.

The usual time for dinner was ten or eleven o'clock in the morning. At that time trestles were brought in and tables arranged along the walls. The rich nobles prided themselves on their gold and silver plate, and silver dishes, cups, and tankards wrought with curious devices glistened on their tables; but in the houses of the less wealthy dishes were often made of wood or pewter. The huge saltcellar was the chief ornament of the table. It was usually of silver and was made in some ornamental shape, sometimes in the form of a stag or some other favorite animal. It had a very important significance, marking the division between the seats of people of rank and those of the common people.

Only knives and spoons were used in eating. Forks did not come into use until quite late in the Middle Ages. Because of the lack of forks there was no easy way of cutting the meat on the plate, so the cutting was done by the carver, who served the meat in small pieces to be taken up with the fingers or on a piece of bread. Soft food was eaten with a spoon. Only one plate and drinking cup was placed for every two people, and it was always a courtesy for a knight and a lady to share the plate and cup.

As soon as the lord entered the hall a horn was sounded, and servitors brought in pitchers, basins, and napkins.

Squires and small pages carried them around to the company, who washed their hands before they sat down to dinner. Then the guests were conducted to their seats at the tables, the places being very strictly assigned according to rank. Those to whom special honor was due were seated

Medieval ladies at table. (From a fifteenth-century manuscript.)

nearest the lord's table, the common folk were placed "below the salt," and the servants at the farthest end of the tables.

A burst of trumpets announced that all were seated; then the master cook entered, closely followed by other servants, bearing huge dishes of smoking viands which were duly pre-

45

sented to everyone in the order of his importance. Soon the tables were groaning under great quantities of food, as the stalwart serving-men carried in course after course from the kitchen.

As there were no napkins, the much-needed basins, pitchers, and towels were passed around again after the meal. Then the guests left the tables, some to stroll in the

A lord and lady in their garden. (From a fifteenth-century manuscript.)

garden. Young knights and ladies loved the open air and the bright sunshine. They would often spend whole afternoons in the pretty walled gardens of the castles, weaving garlands of flowers or conversing in the shade of the trees.

Supper was served at five in the afternoon. At supper the table was adorned with candlesticks of artistic design, but as these were often insufficient to light up the hall, servants sometimes held torches in their hands throughout the meal.

The nobility delighted in giving feasts. Almost any event afforded an excuse for a banquet, and special holidays like Easter, Christmas, Twelfth Night, all were celebrated with elaborate feasts. On such occasions a gay company would gather. The ladies were richly appareled in long robes of beautifully hued silk from the looms of old Cathay, some wrought with gold and silver thread, with long floating sleeves and richly embroidered girdles. The gentlemen were scarcely less brilliant in their long cloaks with rich fur at the neck and wrists, their varicolored hose and long pointed crimson shoes, with heavy gold chains around their necks and jeweled rings on their fingers. Then the old hall, with its timbered rafters from which gay banners hung, its tapestry-hung walls, its stained-glass windows, its tables glittering with gold and silver plate, and many tall tapering candles throwing a mellow light over everything, made indeed a splendid picture.

III

Troubadours and Minstrels

A group of minstrels.

AT THE end of the hall opposite the dais was the minstrels' gallery. A wealthy noble usually had one or more minstrels in his service as part of his household. It was the duty of the musicians to strike up merrily as the attendants carried the dishes into the hall at mealtime and to play and sing between the courses of the meal. Nobles were also in the habit of keeping a fool—or jester—to provide entertainment. He wore a cap and bells and a costume, half of one color and half of another. During meals he told jokes to amuse the

48

company, and his antics and capers were a source of much merriment.

Other entertainment was provided by all sorts of wandering amusement makers, who went about from castle to castle. Jugglers performed marvelous tricks, acrobats tumbled and wrestled, sleight-of-hand performers went through strange feats. The roads of the day were alive with strolling mountebanks and players. Clad in brilliant hues, beribboned and befeathered, they trudged from hall to hall. There were tumblers, tight-rope walkers, stilt walkers, and a host of others. Many and diverse were their accomplishments.

I can play the lute [said the minstrel, Robert Le Maine], the violin, the bagpipe, the syrinx, the harp, the gigne, the gittern, the psaltery, the organistrum, the tabor and the role. I can sing a song well and make tales and fables. I can tell a story against any man, I can make love verses to please young ladies, and can play the gallant for them if necessary. Then I can throw knives into the air and catch them without cutting my fingers. I can do dodges with a string most extraordinary and amusing. I can balance chairs and make tables dance. I can throw a somersault and walk on my head.

After dinner perhaps a poet would entertain the guests with stories or songs, for in castle days people were great lovers of poetry; and as people could not read the storyteller or the reciter of verses was very popular. Many a castle had a poet of its own. There he lived, making and singing beautiful songs. Besides these there were a large number who roamed about the country.

These wandering poet-singers were called by different

names in different places. In southern France they were called troubadours, in northern France trouvères, in Germany minnesingers or meistersingers. There were minstrels of every rank. Some of them were highborn and traveled in state. They sang graceful little songs of love and tales of knightly deeds of valor, accompanying themselves on the lute or some other musical instrument.

One of these little songs begins:

I love the gay spring weather,
And all the trees a-flower,
When a hundred birds together
Make music every hour.

But it sets my heart a-beating
To see the broad tents spread
And bright-armed warriors meeting
And banners floating red.

When camp and street are stirring,
When the city gates stand wide,
When bands of knights are spurring
Through all the countryside . . .

Then the singer goes on, through many verses, describing battles and knightly adventures.

Wherever the troubadour appeared he was sure of a warm welcome and an eager audience. Especially popular were the reciters of romances. These were longer poems

King Arthur's round table.

that clustered around the name of some favorite hero.
Stories of his mighty deeds were told and retold, and with
each telling they grew more and more glorious until the

51

hero became the most noble in spirit, the bravest in heart, of any knight who ever lived. Often the stories were put in verse. These long romances tell of the glory of chivalry, the knight's faith, and the romantic love of the feudal age. All are full of picturesque adventures and present a vivid picture of knighthood.

The people of England loved to listen to stories of King Arthur, who was supposed to have lived in Cornwall on the west coast and to have fought against the Angles and Saxons hundreds of years before the days of the knights. King Arthur was pure in thought and deed and the very ideal of knightly chivalry. The medieval poets told how he had built a great round table at which there was a seat for each of his knights. So they became known as the Knights of the Round Table. King Arthur made his knights solemnly pledge themselves

> *To break the heathen and uphold the Christ,*
> *To ride abroad redressing human wrongs,*
> *To speak no slander, no, nor listen to it,*
> *To honor his own words as if his God's,*
> *To live sweet lives in purest chastity,*
> *To love one maiden only, cleave to her,*
> *And worship her by years of noble deeds*
> *Until they won her.*

The fame of Arthur's court and the deeds of his knights spread far and wide, and many tales grew up about him and his knights of the round table.

In France the greatest hero was Roland, the beloved nephew of Charlemagne. His heroic deeds were told in a long poem called the *Song of Roland*. Charlemagne fought a number of times against the Moors in Spain. In one of his wars, when his army was returning home, Roland was put in charge of the rear guard, which was to follow the main army and protect it from attack.

Roland and his men entered a narrow pass in the Pyrenees, little suspecting that the enemy was near, when suddenly the Moors fell upon them. A terrible battle ensued. Roland and his followers tried to beat them back, but they were greatly outnumbered by the Moors and the struggle was in vain. Roland had a horn, Oliphant, which he was to blow in case of need. His friend Oliver begged him to sound it.

*"Sound Oliphant, Roland, my comrade, and straightway
        shall Charlemagne hear;*
He is threading the mountain gorges, still he is near."

But Roland was too proud to call for help.

*"Nay, God forbid," cried Roland, "that for any heathen
        born*
It shall be said that Roland stooped to sound his horn.
*Shall I be upon the lips of my kinsmen a byword, a shame,
        and a scorn?"*

The battle went on, and at last only a few of his men were left and Roland himself was wounded. Then, yielding to

Oliver's entreaty, Roland blew a blast on his horn. A second time he blew and a third. Faintly the sound reached Charlemagne riding at the head of his army far away. Back hastened the king and his men, and at the sound of the approaching Franks the Moors fled. But Charlemagne was too late; Roland lay dying.

> *"The lord have mercy on thy soul*
> *Never more shall our fair France behold*
> *A knight so worthy, till France be no more,"*

said Charlemagne over the dying Roland.

This stirring poem appealed strongly to the medieval nobles, and wherever men loved brave deeds they sang of Roland, the hero.

The greatest poem of Germany during the Middle Ages was the *Nibelungenlied,* or the song of the Nibelungs. In it were gathered together many ancient legends of the northern peoples. In Germany these tales centered about a fair-haired youth, named Siegfried, who had the courage to conquer all danger. He wooed and married a beautiful princess, named Kriemhild, and with her he lived most happily. But in the end he came to a tragic death, slain by a treacherous enemy, named Hagen. Siegfried had slain the Nibelungs and seized their treasure, together with a magic cloak which rendered its wearer invisible. He had also killed a dragon and by bathing in its blood had become invulnerable except in one place, where a linden leaf touched his body. Hagen

54

killed Siegfried by thrusting a spear in the one place where
he could be hurt.

These are only a few of the many poems and romances
recited and sung by the minstrels which so delighted the
people in castle days. Perhaps you have read some of them,
especially the stories of King Arthur, without knowing that
they have come down to us from the Middle Ages.

IV

Sports and Pastimes

AS TRAVELING was slow and dangerous, and visiting rare, and as but few people could read, various other pastimes were engaged in by the nobles to while away the time. After the evening meal the hall was cleared for dancing, or tables

Hoodman's blind. (From a fourteenth-century manuscript.)

and chairs were brought in for checkers, chess, backgammon, and other games. Grown people in those days also played games that are today played only by children. Hoodman's blind, similar to blindman's buff, was quite a favorite. One of the players was blindfolded, and the others tried to hit him with their hoods without being caught. Hot cockle▪

was also popular. One player knelt, blindfolded, with his head in the lap of another sitting on a stool. Holding his hands behind him, palms up, he cried, "Hot cockles, hot!" The other players in turn struck his hand, and the one kneeling tried to guess who hit him. If he guessed right the striker took his place; if not, he had to pay a forfeit.

Playing bob apple.

A favorite outdoor sport was hunting. About every castle there were tracts of forest and wild moors frequented by bears, deer, wild boar, and other animals. The lord owned all this land, and no one was allowed to hunt in it except at his invitation. When the season permitted, parties of knights dressed in gay cloth suits, with fur-lined capes flung over their shoulders, rode out through the castle gates, carrying

57

stout hunting spears or bows and quivers full of arrows.
With them went the keepers of the hounds, holding the excited dogs, leaping and straining at their leashes. When the
hunting grounds were reached the dogs were turned loose,
and they bounded through the thick underbrush, seeking
the trail of some animal. Perhaps a deer would leap up, and

A hunting scene. (From a fourteenth-century manuscript.)

then like a flash the whole party would go after it, horns
blowing and hounds yelping. Often through the whole day
the hunters scoured the woods, riding over the hills, through
the meadows, and across streams, tracking the game.

Hawking, which was a method of hunting game birds,
was also popular. In every castle an important person was

58

the falconer, whose business it was to catch young hawks and train them. A hawking party would set out on horseback to seek wild birds—quails, pheasants, partridges, or wild

A lord and lady hawking. (From a German manuscript.)

ducks. On the gauntleted wrist of each rider perched his pet hawk—or falcon. Its head was covered with a little hood so that it could not see, and it was held fast to the wrist of its

59

master or mistress by a silver chain attached to its leg. To each leg was also attached a little silver bell engraved with its owner's name, so that if the bird was lost it might be returned by anyone who found it.

When one of the company caught sight of a game bird, he quickly whipped off the hood from his hawk's head and turned it loose. The sharp eyes of the hawk soon saw its prey. With a swift spring it soared high up into the air, its little bells tinkling, and, swooping down on the bird, brought it down. Then the hawk's master blew on a little silver whistle, and the hawk, hearing the call, dropped the bird, flew to his master, and settled again upon his wrist. The game bird was then brought in by the dogs.

Of all the pastimes of the nobles, nothing surpassed in interest the tournaments, which were mimic battles in which they fought one another to exhibit their strength and skill. Knights would often journey long distances to take part in them. Days before a tournament was to be held, the noble giving it sent out invitations, so that all the knights who cared to come might make ready. A herald in his gay livery, accompanied by a trumpeter, set forth, and in every castle yard they came to, the trumpeter blew a blast on his trumpet and the herald made his proclamation, announcing the place and date of the tournament, the conditions of entering it, the prizes to be awarded, and invited the knights to come and exhibit their prowess. As the news spread there were great doings in all the castles for miles about—the polishing of arms and armor, the making of new trappings for the horses, fine new surcoats for the knights, and beautiful costumes for the ladies.

As the time for the tournament approached, the roads of the countryside leading to the castle where it was to be held

A herald announcing a tournament. (From *Tournoi du roi René.*)

were crowded with horsemen and horsewomen, as little parties of knights, accompanied by the ladies of their households, with squires and servants in attendance, made their way to the tilting ground. With a great clatter of hoofs they rode over the drawbridge, through the castle gate, and

51

into the courtyard. Squires and pages from the castle, and even the scullions from the kitchen, hurried out to see the gay procession. The guests were welcomed by the lord of the castle who showed them to the lodgings arranged for them. Many of them who could not find room in the castle set up tents in the meadow near the tilting ground.

Lords and ladies on their way to a tournament. (From *Tournoi du roi René*.)

A level grassy place in a near-by meadow had been fenced into a long oblong shape called the lists, with rows of seats and richly canopied pavilions built for the highborn spectators, decorated with shields and banners and bright with colored hangings. At the center of one of the longer sides

62

was a special gallery for the ladies, in the middle of which was a seat of honor for the Queen of Love and Beauty. The tents of the challengers were pitched at each end, and from each tent fluttered a pennant emblazoned with the coat of arms of the knight who occupied it.

At length the day of the tournament has arrived and the knights are up at dawn and are being carefully dressed and armed by their squires. Trumpets sound, signifying that it is time for the contest to begin, and heralds go through the long avenues of tents calling, "Come forth, knights, come forth!"

Soon a glittering cavalcade is making its way to the lists. Four heralds on foot lead the procession, then come the contestants, two by two, on horseback, each knight followed by his squire. The highly polished armor of the knights gleams in the sunlight, and armorial devices stand out on their shields.

Down one side of the lists and up the other winds the procession, so that all the spectators may see. Then the knights take their stations, half at one end of the lists and half at the other. They hold their lances upright. From the tips of many of them flutter gay ribbons and scarves, tokens worn in honor of their ladies.

The pavilions are filled with ladies in their brilliantly colored gowns and nobles gorgeously arrayed. In other places the humbler onlookers are crowding about the ropes that inclose a part of the lists. The marshal of the tournament takes his place in the middle of the lists, with his assistants—the heralds—who are to keep the score and act as judges, and proclaims silence while the rules are being read, for everything must be done in accordance with the regulations of the tournament.

When all is in readiness there is a grand flourish of trumpets, and the marshal cries, "In the name of God and St. Michael, do your battle!" The heralds shout, "Do your duty, valiant knights!" and from each end of the lists there is a rush of horses, as the two flashing squadrons dash forward with all their might. With helmet closed, and lance lowered, with his shield in front of him to protect his body, each knight bends low in his saddle and charges, trying to strike the shield of his opponent with such force that he unhorses him. Thus, by his skill, he wins the favor of the lady of his choice.

The two sets of horsemen meet in the middle of the lists with a resounding clang of armor, as the spears strike the shields. Horses are thrown back on their haunches and knights sway in their saddles. A fearful cloud of dust rises, almost blinding the contestants. The din of armor, the crash of splintering lances, the excited cries and cheers of the spectators, and the shrill trumpeting of the heralds fill the air. Half the knights on each side have been flung from their horses and are sprawled headlong on the earth with a great clattering of armor. Many are endeavoring to extricate themselves, their squires running up with fresh lances or in other ways attending their masters.

The air is charged with excitement. The spectators, nobles and baseborn alike, leap up and shout and clap their hands. Ladies wave their silken scarves and veils. Each has her

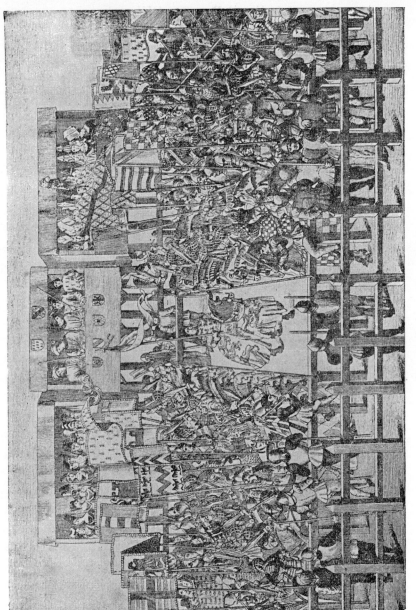

A scene from a tournament.

favorite knight and hopes that he will cover himself with glory. Every now and then a lady in her excitement tears off a girdle or a sleeve from her gown, or a ribbon from her hair, and flings it to her favored champion as his "gage of love," to inspire him to brave deeds in her honor.

The trumpet sounds, and the knights wheel gracefully and canter back to their stations. They take fresh weapons ready for another tilt. There were usually several of such encounters. Sometimes several days were given to these contests. But at length the heralds cry "Fold your banners," and the tournament ends. The gay throng sweeps over the meadow to the castle, leaving the lists deserted.

The tournament was followed by a banquet in the evening. The lord and lady of the castle and all the guests met in the great hall. The lady who had been chosen as the Queen of Love and Beauty took a place upon a dais and a herald led up to her one knight after another, giving the claims of each for a prize. As each one knelt before her she presented to him the reward due him, and with each gift she made a graceful little speech in which she expressed the wish that he would be happy with his ladylove. The knight who had broken the most lances received the first prize. He knelt, and a chaplet of flowers was placed upon his head, the Queen of Love and Beauty saying, "I bestow upon thee this chaplet, Sir Knight, assigned to this day's victor for the deed of valor." The knight kissed the hand of the lady and replied, "The victory was owing to the favor of my lady which I wore." After all the prizes were awarded there was feasting and dancing.

The victor of the tournament receiving the prize. (From *Tournoi du roi René*.)

V

The Christmas Revels

HOLY days were also holidays, and the festivals of the church were celebrated with much merrymaking as well as by religious observances. The Christmas season was a time for feasting and revelry, which cheered the hearts of everyone in the depth of the long dreary winter. At that time all the nobles threw open wide the gates of their castles to their friends, their vassals, and their peasants. Rank and ceremony were forgotten, and all were deemed **equal**, whether lord or serf. Everywhere the old halls were the centers of gay holiday festivities.

Let us visit the hall of a lord in England and see the people of the castle enjoying their Christmas revels. The paneled walls, the minstrels' gallery, and the rafters are all picturesquely decked with holly, ivy, and mistletoe. The vassals and servants of the lord enter the hall to share in the good time.

In preparation for Christmas a huge yule log has been selected, perhaps the whole trunk of a tree. With much shouting and joyous ceremony it is dragged into the hall and placed on the iron dogs in the spacious fireplace. The lord kindles the log from the dying remnant of the old one,

68

A hall in the Middle Ages with the Christmas celebration in full swing.

and the flames go roaring up the chimney. The burning of the yule log was an ancient Christmas custom. It was supposed to bring good luck during the coming year and promise of long feasting. As an accompaniment of the yule log a candle of great size, called the yule candle, burns on the high table, shedding its mellow light on the festive board during the evening.

An enormous feast is served, but first is passed the huge wassail bowl, filled with ale, cider, or wine, spiced and sweetened, with little red apples floating on its surface, and the whole company drinks to one another's health, each one giving the ancient Saxon salute, "Wassail!" which means "To your health," as he presented the bowl to his neighbor, who responded, "Drinkhaile."

Heralded by a jubilant flourish of trumpets, the boar's head, garlanded with sprays of laurel, is brought in, borne shoulder-high on a broad silver platter by the master cook. In its mouth is a roasted apple, and in its ears are sprigs of rosemary. Closely followed by other serving-men carrying smoking dishes, the procession moves slowly to the table, and the whole company rises and joins in singing the *Boar's Head Carol:*

The boar's head in hand bear I,
Bedecked with bays and rosemary:
And I pray you, my masters, be merry
Quot estis in convivio. [So many of you as are at the feast.]

Caput apri defero, [The boar's head I bring,]
Reddens laudes domino. [Rendering praises to the Lord.]

Bringing in the yule log.

The boar's head, as I understand,
Is the rarest dish in all this land,
Which thus bedecked with a gay garland
Let us servire cum cantico. [. . . *serve with a song.*]

When the prodigious appetites of the company have been appeased, fun and jollity of all sorts begin. The company have chosen one of their number to whom is given the title Lord of Misrule, a person dressed in fantastic garb, who is to act as master of ceremonies. He goes about making jokes to amuse the company and seeing that everyone has a good time. He slips a hood over the head of one of the guests and starts the rough old game of hoodman's blind. In another place hot cockles is being played by a group. Still other groups play hunt the slipper, bob apple, and forfeits.

A favorite Christmas sport was snapdragon. A quantity of raisins was deposited in a large dish or bowl and brandy poured over them and ignited. Everyone tried to get a raisin out by plunging his hands into the flames. While this game was going on it was customary to extinguish all the lights so as to get the full effect of the lurid glare of the flaming spirits.

Now comes a loud knocking at the door, and in sweeps a crowd of mummers with their dragon. These were bands of poor men and women who disguised themselves in quaint costumes and masks and went about from castle to castle, singing, dancing, and partaking of the good cheer. They are led by old Father Christmas who enters, saying:

72

The Christmas Revels

Here come I, old Father Christmas.
Welcome, or welcome not,
I hope old Father Christmas
Will never be forgot.

The mummers parade about the hall, amusing the guests by their costumes and their antics, and bow low before the lord and lady of the castle. They act out a play called *St. George and the Dragon,* a rude little drama with plenty of fighting in it. Besides old Father Christmas the characters include, among others, Giant Blunderbore, Little Jack, St. George, old Dr. Ball, and the dragon. Before they give their play, the characters introduce themselves. Giant Blunderbore introduces himself and Little Jack thus:

I am Giant Blunderbore, fee, fi, fum,
Ready to fight ye all—so I says, "Come!"
And this here is my little man Jack,
A thump on his rump and a whack on his back!
[Giving Little Jack two resounding thwacks]
So here I, Blunderbore, takes my stand,
With this little fellow, Jack, at my right hand,
Ready to fight for mortal life. Fee, fi, fum.

Old Dr. Ball introduces himself:

I am the doctor and I cure all ills,
Only gallup my potions, and swallow my pills;

73

I can cure the itch, the stitch, the pox, the palsy and the
     gout,
All pains within and all pains without.
There never was a doctor like Mr. Dr. Ball.

And the dragon introduces himself:

> *I'm the dragon, here are my jaws,*
> *I'm the dragon, here are my claws,*
> *Meat, meat, meat for to eat!*
> *Stand on my head, stand on my feet.*

All the players begin fighting and fall down. Then old Dr. Ball cries:

Get up all, and stand aside,
You have wounded the dragon and finished the fight.

All get up except the dragon, who lies in convulsions on the floor. The doctor forces a large pill down his throat, and with a roar he falls over dead.

After the play the mummers sing, while one of their number goes around the hall with a hat into which the guests throw money.

Sometimes the mummers executed a sword dance if they were sufficiently skillful. Six or more danced in a ring, each holding a wooden sword in his right hand and clasping the tip of his neighbor's with his left. During the dance the swords clashed together rhythmically as a large number of

74

intricate figures were performed, the dancers leaping and twisting in every imaginable way and turning back-somer-saults over the swords or passing under them without break-ing the formation. The dance ended with the interlocking of the swords to form a rose or star, which the leader held aloft in triumph while the whole company cheered.

Thus with songs and dances and merry minstrelsy the happy night was spent. These festivities, under the sway of the jolly Lord of Misrule, did not end with Christmas. They usually continued during the feast of yuletide, which lasted until Twelfth Night, the sixth of January.

Many carols were sung during the festivities of Christmas by the waits who frequented the houses of the gentry at this season. This is one of the old favorites that has come down to us:

> *God rest you merry, gentlemen,*
> *Let nothing you dismay,*
> *Remember Christ our Saviour*
> *Was born on Christmas Day,*
> *To save us all from Satan's pow'r*
> *When we were gone astray.*
>
> *O tidings of comfort and joy, comfort and joy,*
> *O tidings of comfort and joy.*
>
> *In Bethlehem, in Jewry,*
> *This blessed Babe was born,*
> *And laid within a manger,*

Upon this blessed morn;
The which His mother Mary,
Did nothing take in scorn.

From God our heavenly Father,
A blessed angel came;
And unto certain shepherds
Brought tidings of the same:
How that in Bethlehem was born
The Son of God by name.

"Fear not then," said the angel,
"Let nothing you affright,
This day is born a Saviour
Of a pure virgin bright,
To free all those who trust in Him
From Satan's power and might."

The shepherds at those tidings
Rejoicèd much in mind,
And left their flocks a-feeding,
In tempest, storm, and wind:
And went to Bethlehem straightway
The Son of God to find.

And when they came to Bethlehem
Where our dear Saviour lay,
They found Him in a manger,
Where oxen feed on hay;

76

The Christmas Revels

His mother Mary kneeling down,
Unto the Lord did pray.

Now to the Lord sing praises,
All you within this place,
And with true love and brotherhood
Each other now embrace;
This holy tide of Christmas
All other doth deface.

VI

Page, Squire, and Knight

EVERY boy of noble birth had to pass through many years of training before he could become a knight. It began when he was quite a little boy, perhaps not more than seven years old. Sometimes a boy received his training at home, but more often he went to live at the castle of some lord of renown and wealth. Every important noble had several young lads living as pages at his castle.

The pages helped the ladies of the castle in every way they could, and from them they learned many things. Some lady took a special interest in each page, teaching him how to sing and dance, how to compose music and perhaps play upon the harp, and how to make himself agreeable and useful in the castle. She told him stories of knights and heroes, and if she was able to read perhaps she taught him to read.

A quaint little book of medieval manners for the young, called the *Babees Book,* has come down to us, which tells how a page should act. Here are some rules from it:

When you enter your lord's place, say "God Speed" and with humble cheer greet all who are there present. Do not rush in rudely, but enter with head up and at an easy pace, and kneel on one knee only to your lord.

Take no seat, but be ready to stand until you are bidden to sit down. Keep your hands and feet at rest.

Do not lean against a post, in the presence of your lord, or handle anything about the house.

Make obeisance to your lord always when you answer, otherwise stand as still as a stone, unless he speak.

The table manners of the well-bred youth were set forth in the following rules:

Now must I tell you shortly what you shall do at noon when your lord goest to his meat. Be ready to fetch him clear water, and some of you hold the towel for him until he has done. Stand before him until he bids you sit, and be always ready to serve him with clean hands.

Do not hang your head over your dish, or in any wise drink with full mouth.

If you eat with another turn the nicest pieces to him and do not go picking out the finest and largest for yourself.

When ye have done, look then that ye rise up without laughter, or joking, or boisterous word and go to your lord's table, and there stand, and pass not from him until grace be said and brought to an end.

Then some of you should go for water, some hold the cloth, and some pour water upon his hands.

In their spare time, the pages played games, and there was daily exercise in the castle yard. A popular sport, which was training for warfare, was tilting at the quintain. The quintain was the figure of a knight, roughly made of wood, holding a shield in front of him and in his right hand a club. This figure was hung on a pivot fixed to a pole so that

79

it would turn around at a mere touch. Each page, mounted, dashed up to the wooden figure at a gallop and endeavored to strike the shield of the dummy with his lance. If he struck

The game of quintain. The pages ride in turn at the wooden figure of a knight. If the rider strikes the middle of the shield all is well. If he hits it on the side, the figure swings around and strikes him with its club. (From the *Chroniques de Charlemagne*.)

it right in the middle all was well, but if he was clumsy and his aim poor, so that he struck the shield a glancing blow on the side, the figure whirled around as quick as a flash and, to the great delight of all the other pages, gave the

80

unskillful page a stinging blow with its club as he rode by.

For seven years or more a boy lived at a castle as a page. Then he became a squire. A squire was his lord's devoted

A squire being made a knight on the field of battle. (From a medieval manuscript.)

attendant and served him in many ways. He polished his armor, keeping it always bright and shining; he helped care for his horses; he waited upon him at mealtime, carrying water for his hand washing, carving his meat, and filling

81

his cup when it was empty. He rode with his lord to a tournament and to battle, carrying his shield and weapons. If his lord was unhorsed in a tournament the squire rushed in and remounted him; if his lord was wounded in battle he carried him to a place of safety and helped care for his wounds. In the castle yard the squire practiced warlike accomplishments and manly exercises, learning to be at home on a horse's back, to hold his lance correctly, and to manage his shield when his horse was charging. In the society of the ladies of the castle he was always courteous and helpful in every way.

Always the young squire was looking forward longingly to the time when he would become a knight. And when he had mastered his duties, or "won his spurs," by performing some deed proving himself worthy of knighthood, came one of the greatest events of his life, the proud day of his knighting. Sometimes this took place simply on the field of battle, when a squire had shown particular bravery in helping to save his lord's life in time of danger. But ordinarily the knighting was done at the castle and was accompanied by a solemn religious ceremony, each part of which had some significance. First the young aspirant to knighthood took a bath to cleanse him of the blemishes of his past life. Then he must lie down at least for a moment upon a bed, which was to signify "the rest God grants to his followers, the brave knights." Then he put on a snow-white tunic, signifying that "he must keep his flesh from every stain if he would hope to reach heaven." Over this he placed a scarlet robe, to indicate that "he must be ready to pour out

82

his blood for the Holy Church." And finally came a black coat, "to remind him by its somber hue that he must die."

Clad in these garments the young squire, after a long fast, spent the whole night alone in a dark church, lighted only by a single lamp, kneeling in prayer before the high

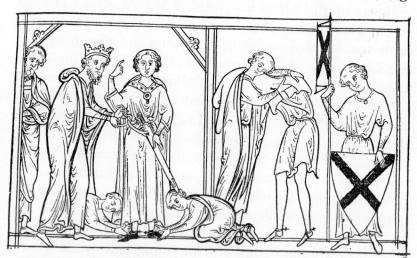

A squire being prepared for the ceremony of knighthood. On the right his coat of mail is being put on, while a squire waits with his shield and banner. At the left a lord is girding on his sword and two pages fasten his spurs. (From a drawing by Matthew Paris, made about 1200.)

altar on which had been placed the new weapons and armor of the knight-to-be, thus consecrating them to God's cause. At daybreak he partook of the Holy Sacrament and was instructed by a priest in the duties of a true knight, and took the solemn vows of chivalry in which he bound himself to be brave and honorable, to maintain the right, to redress

83

wrong, to protect women, to give help to those in trouble, and to show mercy to the weak and defenseless.

Later in the morning he went to the castle courtyard, where were assembled the knights and ladies who had come to grace the occasion of his knighting. First came the ceremony of girding on his armor. The lord, who was to be his godfather in chivalry, belted on his sword with his own hands and buckled on his golden spurs and presented him with his shield. Then the young squire fell upon his knees before his lord; and the lord, striking him lightly on the shoulder with the flat of his sword, pronounced over the kneeling youth the words: "In the name of God, St. Michael, and St. George, I dub thee knight. Be loyal, brave, and true." * Thus the young squire became a knight.

A faultlessly groomed steed, its bridle ornamented with gold, silver, and jewels, was waiting for the newly made knight and presented to him as his charger. Girt in his shining armor, he leaped to the saddle with a bound and gave an exhibition of his skill in riding and in the use of weapons before the assembled company. Then the youth, accompanied by a trusted squire, carrying his shield and helmet and an armful of lances, rode out over the drawbridge in quest of adventure and renown, seeking by some knightly deed to prove his valor and win the love of a fair lady. Perhaps the young knight might find some damsel in distress and rescue her; perhaps he might seek out another knight and challenge him to joust with him.

---

* St. Michael was the prince of the celestial armies and vanquisher of evil. St. George was a Christian hero of the fourth century.

The degradation of a knight. If a knight broke his vow or was guilty of some grave breach of knightly honor, he was publicly disgraced.

The ideals of the knights were represented by their idea of chivalry. The true knight was expected to be loyal to the church and to his overlord, to be just and pure, to speak only the truth, to champion the right, to be fair even to his enemies, to be kind and generous to all in distress, to know no fear, to protect women and the helpless. His honor was his most priceless jewel.

These ideals of chivalry set a high standard of conduct for the nobles. Many knights were unable to live up to them. If a knight broke his vows, or was guilty of some grave breach of knightly honor, he was publicly disgraced. On a post was hung the shield of the erring knight, upside down and smeared with paint. Heralds led him forth and stripped one piece after another of his armor from him. His shield was broken to pieces, his spurs were cut off, his sword was broken over his head. Then the poor wretch was laid in a coffin and dragged to the church, where the priests chanted the funeral service over him just as if he were dead, for he was considered "dead to honor."

not cultivate the
ded. They spent
asting, jousting,
fe of gentlemen.
n as degrading
:.

nged to the lord
ed a manor. On
ood and other
l his retinue of
nobles to live
s these estates

lage clustered
. Their houses
rough plaster
ed earth, and
ey. A fire was
e drifted up
joined to the

Serfs receiving
fifteenth-century

house, and th
under the sam

Around ev

VII

Tillers of the Soi_

THE nobles did no useful work. They did
fields, and they made nothing that they nee
their time, as we have seen, in fighting, f
and in other ways considered fitting the li
Any kind of useful work was looked up
and beneath the dignity of highborn peopl

All the land for miles around a castle belo
of the castle. This vast feudal estate was cal
the land toiled the peasants, raising the
things needed by the lord and his family an
armed men, thus making it possible for the
and devote their time to fighting. Sometim
were called vills, and the peasants villeins.

The homes of the peasants made a little vi
about a green just outside the wall of the castle
were tiny, low, one-roomed cottages, built of
and thatched with straw, with a floor of pack
one little window. There was usually no chimr
built in the middle of the floor, and the smo
through a hole in the roof. Often a shed was

their lord's orders before going to work. (From a manuscript.)

cattle and sheep of the peasants were almost
e roof with them.

ry castle lay great stretches of land. A portion

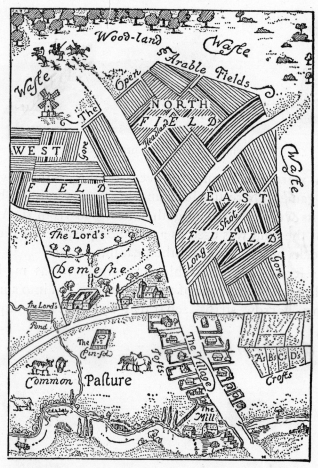

The plan of a medieval manor. Certain strips are blackened to show that they all belonged to the same peasant. (From an old drawing.)

of the estate, called the lord's domain, was reserved by the lord for his own use. Part of this was left as wild forests,

89

Plowing. (From the Luttrell *Psalter*.)

which were the haunts of deer, rabbits, wild hogs, and
other game. There the lord and his guests hunted, but the
peasants were allowed to gather firewood from it. Another
part of the land was used as a common pasture for the herds
and flocks of the lords and the peasants.

The fertile land, suitable for farming, was made into
three big fields, each one of which was divided into a number
of long, narrow strips, separated by ridges of unplowed

Sowing the seed.

Gathering the sheaves.

land. In the fall one field was planted with wheat, rye, or some other grain. In the spring the second field was planted

Driving a harvest cart uphill. (From the Luttrell *Psalter.*)

91

with oats or barley. The third field was unplanted. The next year the empty field of the year before was seeded with wheat, the old wheat field with oats, while the oat field was left vacant. If the same field is planted year after year the soil becomes poor. As medieval farmers did not know how to enrich their soil, they rotated their crops in this way, always leaving one field vacant so that the soil might become fertile by itself.

The methods of farming were the same as those that had been in use for centuries. In the spring the peasants plowed the land with their big, clumsy plows, drawn by slow-moving oxen; then they harrowed it and sowed it. In the fall they reaped the grain with sickles, bound it into sheaves, piled them high on carts, and hauled them to the lord's barn. There they spread the grain on the floor and beat out the heads with long jointed clubs called flails.

With such poor methods of farming the peasants were always busy with their backbreaking work, in order to raise enough food for all the people of the castle. Day in, day out, rain or shine, in the cold of winter and the heat of summer, they rose early and worked late, their wives and daughters helping with the lighter tasks.

Not all the peasants worked on the land. Some were shepherds, who protected the herds of sheep from wild animals as they cropped the grass in the meadows. Some were swineherds, who watched the hogs as they rooted for acorns among the leaves and underbrush in the woods. There were some skilled artisans among the peasants—the smith, the carpenter, the shoemaker, and others. In the

92

castle were cooks and all kinds of servants to do the household work. There was the miller who ran the lord's mill, the

Shepherds. The shepherd sitting under the tree is playing his pipe. The shepherd dogs have been trained to know what the different notes on the pipe mean as signals in rounding up the sheep.

93

vintner who made the wine, and the brewer who made the ale and beer.

The peasants were not paid for their work. Instead each peasant had a certain number of strips of land on which he could raise his own crops. These strips were scattered through the fields, a strip here and a strip there. As some parts of the land were better than others, it was divided up in this way so that the good and bad land would be divided fairly among the peasants. This arrangement was not a very good one, however, because a peasant wasted a good deal of time going about from one of his strips to another.

In return for the use of the land the peasant owed his lord many services. For at least three days a week he had to work on his lord's land under the watchful eye of the overseer, whose business it was to see that the work was properly done. The rest of the time the peasant was free to work on his own land. But at harvest time the lord received a part of the grain raised by the peasants on their land. The peasant could grind his grain at his lord's mill, but each time he had to leave a portion of the ground grain for his lord. He could have his bread baked in the oven which belonged to his lord, but out of each baking he must leave a loaf for his lord.

All the good things produced by the toil of the peasants went to the tables of the feudal lords. In contrast to their sumptuous diet the food of the peasants was poor and coarse. They lived mainly on fish, salt pork, soup, coarse black bread, cheese, and porridge. Sometimes a daring peasant might poach on his lord's hunting grounds, but this

94

was very dangerous, for if a peasant was caught with a hare or a haunch of venison, he was severely punished.

The peasants had few rights. They could not own any property. They were bound to the soil. When a noble acquired an estate he received the serfs with it just as he got the trees that grew on it. They had to obey their lords in all things. They could not marry without their lord's consent. They could not leave the estate without their lord's permission, and it was an almost unheard-of thing for a peasant to leave a manor. For one thing, it was too dangerous. There were few roads in the forests surrounding the castles, and in the woods lurked robbers ready to pounce on anyone who came by. The serfs would not have dared to set off on foot through this dangerous wilderness even if their lords had allowed them to do so. Few peasants, therefore, knew anything of the world beyond their own manor, and very seldom did they see anybody they had not known all their lives.

The life of the peasants was indeed hard. Living in wretched hovels, they were able to win by the hardest labor little more than the barest necessities, and the world offered them little hope of a better condition. Writers of the time comment on their misery. In the *Vision of Piers Plowman*, written in 1362 by William Langland, we get a pitiful picture of the English peasants:

> *What they win by their spinning to make their*
> *porridge with,*
> *Milk and meal to satisfy the babes—*
> *The babes that continually cry for food—*

95

This they must spend on the rent of their houses,
Ay, and themselves suffer with hunger,
With woe in winter rising a-nights
In the narrow room to rock the cradle.

Pitiful it is to see the cottage-women's woe,
Ay, and many another that puts a good face on it,
Ashamed to beg, ashamed to let the neighbors know
All that they need, noontide and evening.
Many the children and nought but a man's hands
To clothe and feed them; and a few pennies come in,
And many mouths to eat the pennies up.
Bread and thin ale for them are a banquet,
Cold flesh and cold fish are like roast venison,
A farthing's worth of mussels, a farthing's worth
     of cockles
Were a feast for them on Friday or fast days.

So generation after generation of peasants lived and
worked as their forefathers had lived and worked before
them. For centuries the lowly serfs accepted their hard lot
without question. They knew nothing different, and it never
occurred to them that any other fate was possible for them.

VIII

Peasant Pleasures

A group of morris dancers.

ALTHOUGH the lives of the peasants were hard and monotonous there were some bright spots to relieve their ceaseless round of toil. Sometimes there was a fair at a neighboring town which they were permitted to attend. Sometimes a group of jugglers on their way to a castle stopped at a village and showed their tricks. There was occasionally a strolling minstrel for the common people, too. He wandered about, dressed in his bright-hued jacket with a long peacock's feather stuck in his cap and a viol slung on

97

his back. At a village green he would unsling his viol and begin strumming the strings, and soon the peasants would be crowding about to hear him sing some well-known ballad. After the performance he would collect offerings from his audience. Then he would start off again, perhaps to a near-by fair, where the merrymakers would flock about him. It was a carefree, roving life.

Many of these minstrels in England sang ballads telling of the adventures of the famous outlaw, Robin Hood, in Sherwood Forest. According to tradition Robin Hood was of noble birth. He was supposed to be the Earl of Huntingdon. His name was associated with the beautiful lady Matilda Fitzwater, known as Maid Marian. Their marriage was prevented by a charge of treason brought against the young earl. Then he fled to Sherwood Forest to become the outlaw Robin Hood. Here he was followed by others who linked their fortunes with his. His band grew in numbers until a hundred or more followers acknowledged him as their leader.

Never were such merry men as those who roamed through the greenwood with Robin Hood. Among them were Little John, Will Scarlet, Friar Tuck, and Alan-a-Dale. They passed the time in games of archery. No archer ever lived who could send an arrow with such skill as could Robin Hood.

Robin and his band despoiled barons, abbots, and knights of their wealth, and with it they gave help to those who were in need or in trouble. He was pictured as the most humane of outlaws, bold and fair in fight, courteous and kind to women and children, and bountiful to the poor and needy. Thus he came to be looked upon by the poor people as their champion.

We do not know surely whether Robin Hood really lived or not. It may be that he really was a nobleman whose lands had been taken away from him, but possibly many of his adventures may have happened to other men living in forests. Probably among these outlawed men there was one who distinguished himself for his daring and courage. The people liked Robin so well that they made him the hero of the adventures that happened to all the others. Stories of his brave deeds were eagerly taken hold of by the ballad makers and turned into verse, in which Robin was given all the qualities that endeared him to the people. For hundreds of years many ballads about Robin Hood were sung by minstrels in England. Here is one of them:

Robin Hood and the Bishop

Come, gentlemen all, and listen a while
And a story to you, I'll unfold;
I'll tell you how Robin Hood served the bishop,
When he robbed him of his gold.

As it fell out on a sunshiny day,
When Phoebus was in his prime,
Then Robin Hood, that archer good,
In mirth would spend some time.

And as he walked the forest along,
 Some pastime for to spy,
Then was he aware of a proud bishop
 And all his company.

"O, what shall I do?" said Robin Hood then,
"If the bishop he doth take me,
 No mercy he'll show unto me, I know.
Therefore away I'll flee."

Then Robin was stout, and turned him about,
And a little house there he did spy;
 And to an old wife for to save his life,
He loud began to cry.

"Why, who art thou?" said the old woman.
"Come tell to me for good."
"I am an outlaw, as many do know,
 My name, it is Robin Hood.

"And yonder's the bishop and all his men,
 And if that I taken be
Then day and night, he'll work me spite
And hanged I shall be."

"If thou be Robin Hood," said the old woman,
"As thou dost seem to be,
 I'll for thee provide, and thee I will hide
From the bishop and his company.

"*For well I remember, one Saturday night,*
Thou brought'st me both shoes and hose;
Therefore I'll provide, thy person to hide,
And keep thee from thy foes."

"*Then give me soon thy coat of gray,*
And take thou my mantle green,
Thy spindle and twine unto me resign
And take thou my arrows so keen."

The bishop he came to the old woman's house,
And he called with a furious mood,
"*Come let me see, and bring unto me,*
That traitor, Robin Hood."

The old woman he set on a milk-white steed,
Himself on a dapple gray;
And for joy he had got Robin Hood,
He went laughing all the way.

But as they were riding, the forest along,
The bishop he chanced for to see,
A hundred brave bowmen, stout and bold,
Stood under the greenwood tree.

"*O who is yonder?*" *the bishop then said,*
"*That's ranging within yonder wood?*"
"*Marry,*" *says the old woman,* "*I think it to be*
A man called Robin Hood."

"Why, who art thou?" the bishop he said,
"Which I have here with me?"
"Why, an old woman, thou lordly bishop;
Lift up my cap and see."

"Then woe is me," the bishop he said,
"That ever I saw this day!"
He turned him about; but Robin stout,
Call'd to him and bid him stay.

Robin Hood took his mantle from his back,
And spread it upon the ground,
And out of the bishop's portmanteau
He soon told five hundred pound.

"Now let him go," said Robin Hood;
Said Little John, "That may not be;
For I vow and protest, he shall sing us a mass,
Before that he go from me."

Then Robin Hood took the bishop by the hand,
And bound him fast to a tree,
And made him sing a mass
To him and his yeomandree.

On holidays and feast days the peasants took part in merrymaking and sports on the village green. Of all the holidays May Day was nearest to the poor people's hearts, especially in England, when, after the long bleak winter,
102

May Day in England.

springtime dawned with all its brightness and beauty. We can well imagine their joy at the approach of spring, when the fields, for months bare and desolate, were once more clothed in green, the birds returned to sing among the branches of the trees, young lambs were frisking in the meadows, flowers were in bud and blossom, making the land a tapestry of white and pink and yellow.

Long before the break of day troops of merrymakers—young lads and lasses, milkmaids, shepherds and plowmen, old men and their wives—left their thatch-roofed cottages and hastened to the woods to gather the blooming hawthorn and other spring flowers, and, laden with their spoil, returned before the sun rose. Some of them became walking bowers, having adorned themselves with leaves and flowers, or jacks-in-the-green, incased in tall frames of herbs and posies with flags at the top. With merry shouts and horn blowings, they threaded their way through blossoming lanes to the village and danced through each house and adorned every door and window with fresh boughs.

The greatest treasure brought back from the woods was the Maypole, drawn by several yoke of oxen, each with a sweet nosegay of flowers tied to the tip of his horns. In a gay procession the whole village escorted the flower-decked pole, with music, song, and rejoicing, to the village green.

In the procession there was sure to be a man dressed in a green tunic, bearing a magnificent bow, with bugle horn hung around his neck, representing Robin Hood, the beloved outlaw and friend of the poor and distressed, who had taken such strong hold on the affections of the people. By his side, attended by some maidens, walked Maid Marian in a white dress, Friar Tuck in russet gown and with his ponderous staff, Little John, and other companions of the famous outlaw.

Amid shouts and laughter and bursts of song the young men raise the massive pole, garlanded with flowers and bound with gay streamers from top to bottom, with banners floating from its top. The villagers seize the flying streamers, and young and old dance about the pole to music supplied by the pipe and tabor, or tunes played by the village fiddler.

A girl was chosen to be Queen of the May, very often Maid Marian, to preside over the ceremonies; an arbor of boughs was made for her, decked with flowers; and a man was made Lord of the May to assist her. Usually this was none other than Robin Hood.

All day long there are games and revels. Targets are set up, and Robin Hood and his archers give an exhibition of their skill. There is a close contest of archery, and after many shots the winner is crowned with a laurel wreath. Short plays are given, introducing the chief exploits of Robin and his band. Dancers and jugglers show their tricks. A company of morris dancers, clad in green and yellow, decorated with gay scarves and ribbons, with bright-colored handkerchiefs tied around their necks, dance their lively measures, said to have been introduced from Moorish Spain. At their knees they wore pads of bells tuned to different notes, so as to sound in harmony as they danced, and they carried sticks and handkerchiefs which they used in their dances. With them they had a hobbyhorse. This was a man

105

in a light wooden framework representing a horse, covered with trappings hanging to the ground to prevent the man's feet from being seen. During the morris dances the hobbyhorse pranced and curvetted to the great joy of the crowd. A formidable dragon approaches, hisses, and flaps his wings, which makes the hobbyhorse kick and rear frantically. A jester contributes his share to the mirth.

So all day long the villagers play, and dance, and sing, joyously welcoming the spring.

The Medieval Church

IX

The Age of Great Faith

PERHAPS the greatest legacy which Rome left to the world
was the Roman church, which spread throughout Europe
and profoundly influenced the lives of people for centuries
after the splendor of Rome itself had passed away. You
know, perhaps, that in the days of the Roman Empire Jesus
was born in Palestine, a little country at the eastern end of
the Mediterranean Sea. As he grew to manhood, he began
preaching a new religion of peace and love and brotherly
kindness. In those days Palestine was ruled by the Romans;
and the Roman government, fearing the spread of these new
ideas, forbade the Christians to worship and began punish-
ing those who disobeyed. Many Christians were cast into
prison, others were burned at the stake, still others were
thrown to wild beasts in the Colosseum. Their churches
were torn down, and often they had to worship in secret—
in underground passages called catacombs. Many of these
can still be seen today under the streets of Rome.

In spite of terrible persecution the new religion continued
to spread. Then after about three hundred years there came
a Roman emperor, named Constantine, who became a
Christian. After that Christians no longer had to worship
in secret. Thus Christianity, which had been the religion

of a small group of people who had been cruelly persecuted for their faith, became the religion of the Roman Empire.

To the head of the church was given the name Pope, which means father, and it was his duty to look after the

A bishop ordaining a priest.

affairs of the church just as a father would look after those of his family. Under the Pope were archbishops and bishops, each of whom ruled over an important district of the church. Below the bishops and archbishops were the parish priests, of whom there was one or more in every village.

110

The Age of Great Faith

Among the last words of Christ to his followers were, "Go ye into all the world, and preach the gospel to every creature." So zealous Christian missionaries journeyed to the far corners of Europe to spread their religion among the barbarous tribes. By the time the barbarians settled down in the various countries most of them had given up their early, heathen religion and had adopted the Christian faith.

A lovely little story has come down to us as to how the Christian religion was first carried to Britain. It is said that one day when Pope Gregory was a young man he was passing through the market place of Rome and came to a spot where some fair-haired boys were huddled together waiting to be sold as slaves. Their faces were beautiful, their eyes were blue, and their hair was light and fine and soft. Never before had Gregory seen such handsome youths.

"From what country do these boys come?" asked Gregory.

"From the island of Britain," was the answer.

"Are they Christians?" he asked.

He was told that they were still heathens. Then he asked to what nation they belonged.

"They are called Angles," replied their owners.

"They should be angels, not Angles," said Gregory, looking at their lovely faces, "for they have the faces of angels."

In after years Gregory remembered the fair-haired captives of the market place and sent Augustine, a learned and pious monk, to Britain to preach the gospel to the people. Augustine built a monastery where the Cathedral of Canterbury now stands. Other missionaries worked in other parts

111

of England. Thus the English were gradually converted to the Christian faith.

Pope Gregory the Great sending out missionaries.

By the eleventh century most of western Europe had been converted to Christianity. So to the church, as organized by Rome, the word catholic, which means universal, came to be applied, for this church was, for centuries, the only church in all the countries of civilized Europe, and all the people, except the Jews, were members of it.

The church was the greatest unifying and civilizing force in the world during the Middle Ages. It aimed to unite all people into one Christian brotherhood. There was one faith, one religious service for everybody, one set of rules for the way people should live. It taught that all men—the humblest serf and the proudest knight—were equal before God, and to all men who lived good lives it offered the same reward— happiness in the life to follow. It played a part in every important phase of people's lives, from the cradle to the grave. Shortly after birth a person was baptized in the church, at its altar he was married, and when he died the church administered the last rites through which he was to come into the life hereafter.

Religion gave comfort and hope to the poor and downtrodden and helped the poor people to endure their hard lot. They thought that things were as they were because God willed it so. The Bible itself said, "The poor ye have always with you," and they accepted their unhappy fate as a stage in a journey toward a better world after death.

The church protected the weak and stood for peace and right living. Through what was called the right of sanctuary it protected fugitives from pursuit by an enemy, to show that the Christian religion stood for mercy. A person accused of crime, who fled to a church and took refuge within its consecrated walls, secured safety for a certain length of time. It was considered a sin against God to drag even a criminal from the altar. This was an excellent pro-

113

vision in times when there was little real law. It served to check violence and bloodshed by giving time for angry passions to cool. Those who visit Durham Cathedral in England today can still see the knocker which a fleeing person used to gain entrance there. When this was sounded the door was opened by a porter who lived in a little room above the door.

The knocker on the sanctuary door at Durham Cathedral.

As time passed the church became a vast organization of great power. It taught what was right and wrong in all matters of conduct, and everyone accepted what it taught without question. Everyone was subject to the rules, the high and powerful as well as the poor and lowly, for the church was above the greatest nobles and even kings. Anyone who

114

disobeyed its regulations might be punished by excommunication, which was the most dreaded punishment known. It cut off the offender from all Christian fellowship. No one might speak to him, feed him, or shelter him. He could not attend religious services nor receive the sacrament, and if he died unforgiven he could not receive a Christian burial and his soul was thought to be lost. Even the highest noble feared the power of the church which could thus close the gates of heaven to him.

By the interdict a whole community, or even a whole country, might be cut off from the church. Then all religious rites ceased. The churches were all closed. Babies could not be baptized, no marriage rites could be performed, and all the people of the afflicted region dressed like penitents and prayed for the removal of the curse.

Nowhere in the world today does the church wield such widespread influence and authority as the Roman Catholic Church did from the fifth to the fifteenth centuries.

X

Sermons in Stone

IT WAS at this time of the flowering of the Christian faith that there began to rise all over Europe magnificent cathedrals, those marvels of construction which still today fill the eye of the beholder with wonder and admiration. High, tapering spires on many carry the eye heavenward, as if their builders meant to draw men's thoughts to the things above this earth. The horizontal flat-topped towers of others give one the idea of the heavenly peace promised man after his earthly life. On entering their dim and lovely interiors one seems to leave behind the noise and turmoil of the everyday world, and to feel a sense of uplifting solemnity, as if one were treading on holy ground.

France led the way in building cathedrals. The architecture of the earliest medieval churches resembled that of Rome and is known as Romanesque. The roofs were usually made of stone, and many pillars were needed to hold up these heavy roofs. These pillars were connected by round arches of stone above them. It was also necessary to make the walls of the churches very thick to support the roofs, and the windows of the churches had to be quite small so that the walls would not be weakened.

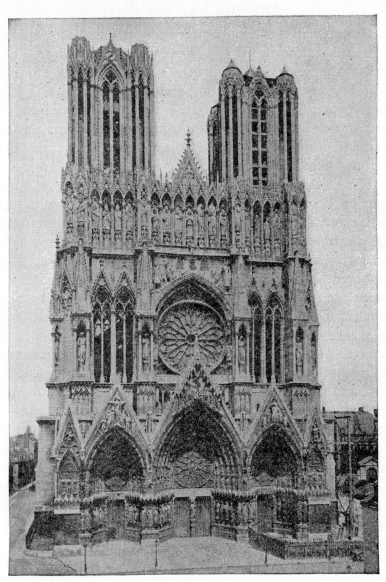

The cathedral at Rheims.

The architects of France were not satisfied with this way of building, and in the twelfth century they devised a new and wonderful way of constructing their churches. This new type of architecture was called Gothic, which was a term of reproach applied to it by Italian architects, who did not like it and still clung to the architecture of the ancient Romans. They thought of the people to the north as still barbarous Goths and called their style of churches Gothic.

The Gothic architects wanted to keep the curved stone roof but to do away with the thick, solid walls, with only little narrow slits for windows, which made the interior of the churches dark and gloomy. To do this they invented a new way of supporting the weight of the roof. They gathered the weight at certain points by using arches and supporting the arches by pillars. To help the walls bear the burden of the roof they braced them at certain points with solid masses of masonry, called buttresses, outside the church. These buttresses were connected above by means of flying buttresses with the points where the arches of the roof had the greatest tendency to push outward. In this way the stone roof could be supported without thick, massive walls. When the walls were no longer needed to support the roof, they could be made thinner and the wall spaces filled with high, wide windows.

From France the Gothic style spread to Germany, England, and Spain. As time went on each nation developed its own style, and by the end of the thirteenth century the buildings of all northern Europe were Gothic. But it was in France that this new architecture reached its highest per-

118

A stained-glass window in Chartres Cathedral.

fection. The cathedrals at Chartres, Amiens, Rheims, are among the great Gothic buildings of the world. That at Chartres is perhaps the finest of all, with its sculpture, the most beautiful since Greek times, and the loveliest stained glass in the world. In Germany the cathedrals of Cologne and Strassburg are the best. One of the most perfect of the English cathedrals is that at Salisbury. No one has ever been able to build more beautiful churches than these, and up to the present time almost all our church architecture has imitated them.

In many places there was no stone for the building of the cathedral, and it had to be hauled from distant places. Thousands of people, even those of high rank, harnessed themselves to the heavy carts and dragged the stone from the quarries, and the other materials needed for the building. For miles around, the roads would be thronged with processions of men and women, tugging at the long ropes by which they dragged the slow-moving carts over the rough roads.

Who has ever heard tell in times past [says an old account] that powerful princes of the world, that men brought up in honor and wealth, that noble men and women, have bent their proud and haughty necks to the harness of carts, and that, like beasts of burden, they have dragged stone, cement, wood to build the abode of Christ? And while men of all ranks drag the heavy loads—so great the weight that sometimes a thousand are attached to each wagon—they march in such silence that not a murmur is heard. When they halt on the road nothing is heard but the confession of sins and

120

Glass making.

prayers to God. They forget all hatred, discord is thrown far aside, and the unity of hearts is established. When they have reached the church they arrange the wagons about it and during the whole night they celebrate the watch with hymns and canticles.

Year after year the work went on. The construction of a cathedral sometimes extended over two or three centuries. One generation planned it and began the building, and another finished the work.

How proud the people were of the churches they were building, and how they loved to beautify them! All over Europe a host of workmen were happy to have a part in so glorious a work, each man laboring joyously to perfect every part of God's dwelling. The great lofty windows were filled with stained glass of exquisite colors, all fitted together like a mosaic. The glass workers, particularly of France, brought their art to the greatest perfection. It is more beautiful than the finest modern work. First they drew the design for the window, indicating with heavy black lines the iron bars necessary to hold the window firmly. Then they cut out tiny pieces of glass, a separate piece for each color, and bound them together with strips of lead. Thus bit by bit they built up their design of a window.

When the sunlight filtered through the bits of glass they shone like beautifully colored jewels—the deep red of rubies, the blue of sapphires, the green of emeralds, and so on. Saints of devout mien appeared in many of the windows, angels of joyful aspect in others, or shepherds attending their flocks by night, or the Wise Men following the star

122

The arches around the doorways were ornamented with saints and angels and scenes from the Bible.

in the East till it led them to the manger in Bethlehem. These "storied windows" were the glory of the Gothic cathedrals. They were the picture books of the period when few people could read. Medieval boys and girls, though they never learned to read or write, could learn the Bible story by looking at them.

The arches of the doorways were ornamented with figures of saints and angels and apostles and scenes from the Bible. The tops of the pillars were beautifully carved with foliage, sometimes looking more like lacework than stone. Here and there the artist stonecutters might introduce amusing faces or animals. So side by side with saints and angels are often found little goblins, strange beasts, and other creations of medieval fancy.

On the roofs grotesque stone figures, in the form of demons, fantastic animals, or birds, were often placed. Through the mouths of these strange-looking creatures the rain water from the roof spouted out clear of the building. They were called gargoyles, which means throats, because of the gurgling noise which the water made when passing through them. These fabulous monsters were found to be so decorative that they were often used merely as ornaments which never carried water. The gargoyles and other comic figures on the roof of Notre Dame in Paris are especially famous. Many of them are perched up on parapets, leaning over the corners, and seem to be looking down and grinning at the people far below.

The wood carvers also had much to do with beautifying the churches. The Gothic artisans were marvelous woodworkers, and their exquisite carving enriched the choirs and the pulpit. No two carvings were alike. The wood carvers found inspiration in the world about them, in the everyday occupations of the people, in the forms of animals, in the faces of men, and in the events of daily life. Sometimes they

Gargoyles often decorated the roofs of cathedrals. The two pictured here are perched on the roof of Notre Dame Cathedral in Paris.

gave rein to their humorous fancy by carving some droll little figure.

Today we marvel at the creations of the workmen of those days. They put their hearts and souls into their work, building into stone, and wood, and glass their faith, their hope, their aspirations, their dreams of justice, and their vision

125

of beauty. The result is some of the finest work ever done by man.

On Sundays and holy days the church was aglow with light and beauty. A profusion of candles burned in every little alcove before every shrine and image, and the high altar at the front was ablaze with tapering archeries of light from tall candles set in wrought-gold candlesticks. Above all a great golden crucifix, thickly set with precious jewels, gleamed.

In slow procession the priests move toward the altar in their richly embroidered vestments, through long lines of humbly kneeling worshipers. Choir boys in scarlet and lace walk slowly, swinging their censers of perfume-bearing incense. Beautiful banners and crosses are borne aloft. Thus the solemn mass proceeds, with pomp and ceremony, with the fragrance of incense, the silver sound of tinkling bells, the kneelings and uprisings, and over all the rhythmic chanting in Latin by the priests. And ever and again the deep full notes of the organ mingle with the joyous voices of the choir, as they lift up their praises to God.

On festival days, such as Christmas and Easter, the service, always so splendid and impressive, was made even more so by little dramas acted by the priests and accompanied by beautiful singing. On the holy Christmas eve a cradle was placed upon the high altar and near by an image of the Virgin Mary. From a lofty place above the choir a sweet-faced choir boy, dressed as an angel, announces to some priests below, as they enter the church in the character of shepherds, the glad tidings of the birth of Christ: "Fear not,

126

for behold, I bring you good tidings of great joy, which shall be to all people. For unto you is born this day in the city of David a Savior, which is Christ the Lord. And this shall be a sign unto you: Ye shall see the babe wrapped in swaddling clothes, lying in a manger."

Other choir boys, stationed aloft, break out into a joyous hymn of praise:

Glory to God in the highest, and on earth peace, good will to men.

The priests, as the shepherds, carrying their crooks in their hands, move toward the altar, chanting in Latin as they go, "Let us go even unto Bethlehem to see this thing which the Lord hath made known to us."

As they reach the altar the shepherds halt before the cradle, and there are met by two priests who say to them in Latin, "Whom seek ye in the manger, shepherds, say?"

To whom the shepherds reply, "The savior, Christ, the Lord, a babe wrapped in swaddling clothes, according to the words of the angel."

The priests then show them the child, saying, "The child is here, with Mary, his mother, concerning whom the prophet Isaiah foretold."

The shepherds, after adoring the holy babe, depart, singing, "Alleluia! Alleluia! Now we know the truth that Christ is born on earth!"

Thus the story of the birth of Christ was acted out in the medieval church. At Easter the dialogue between the angel and the three women at the holy sepulcher afforded another opportunity for acting out a story. By thus presenting scenes from the Bible in dramatic form the priests sought to impress them upon the minds of their simple-minded flocks by bringing before their very eyes the persons and scenes recorded in the holy Scriptures. And there is no doubt that these living pictures did for the people what no mere reading of the words ever could have done.

By degrees these simple little scenes and acted bits grew longer and fuller until the whole Bible story was told. And as they became more and more elaborate more space was needed for them than the church offered and for the crowds of people that flocked to the services. A scaffolding was therefore built on the church steps, and the audience occupied the churchyard or the square in front of the church. The upper step of the church represented heaven, a few steps lower down the earth, and lower still was hell.

By and by these acted scenes left the church entirely and were given by the guilds. We shall tell about that later on in the book when we come to the life of the tradesmen in the towns.

XI

Within Monastery Walls

IN THE early Middle Ages, when invasions and warfare were filling the world with violence and bloodshed, some devout men felt that the world was so wicked that they must withdraw from it. Often they went into deserted places and lived alone in caves as hermits, spending their time in fasting and prayer. There also grew up all over Europe communities of men and women in monasteries and convents, who took vows to live lives of self-denial, to give up the pleasures of the world, and devote themselves to the service of God and their fellow men. In time every country of western Europe was dotted with monasteries and convents.

A monastery was usually built around an enclosed space, called a cloister. All around the four sides of this open court with a lawn in the center, where often a fountain played, was a covered passageway where the monks could come for quiet walks when their work for the day was done. On one side were rows of long narrow alcoves—or cells—where the monks slept, just large enough for a cot and a table and chair, and lighted only by a narrow window. On another was the long dining hall, or refectory, where the monks took their meals, on another the chapel, and on the fourth the library and writing room.

Near the cloister were the workshops for spinning, weaving, dyeing, the bake ovens, blacksmith shops, and shops for other kinds of work, for everything used in the monastery was made by the monks. Outside the wall of the monastery were the fields and woodlands and meadowlands. Here the monks raised their food and kept their cattle and sheep.

When a man became a monk he took three vows. He vowed never to marry, never to own worldly goods, and to obey the rules and regulations of the monastery. He was allowed to live in the monastery a year before taking these vows, but once he had taken them he could never go back to the ordinary life of the world but must remain a monk for the rest of his days.

The monks lived together in loving equality, calling one another "brother." From among their number they chose one to be the head of the monastery, whom they called "Father," who ruled his large family gently, but justly and firmly.

In contrast to the elaborate dress of most men of the time the monks wore long loose robes of coarse stuff, tied about the waist with a cord, with cowls—or hoods—which could be pulled up over the head when needed. Nor did they have rich food. There were but two meals a day in the monasteries, and the food was of the simplest—no meat, perhaps eggs, fish or fowl, bread and vegetables, and a little fruit. The monks partook of their meals in silence, or listened to

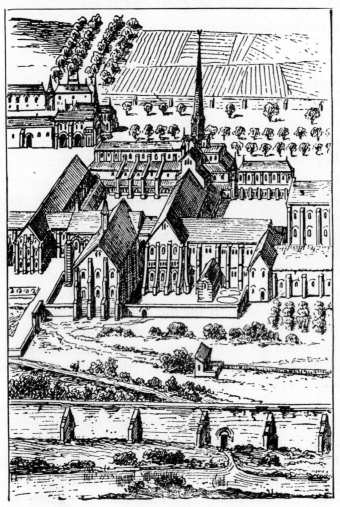

A medieval monastery.

one of the brothers who read aloud to them from some holy book.

Much time was spent in the church of the monastery. Long before the sun was up the monks began their devotions. Seven times during the day the chapel bell rang, and the monks gathered in the church and sang psalms and offered up prayers. Shortly after midnight, the bell sounded again, and they rose from their hard cots and once more made their way to the church to chant the mass. They also spent hours in meditation each day and in reading the Bible or the lives of the saints.

Each monk did some useful work. Some plowed the fields and planted and harvested the grain, some tended the sheep and milked the cows and made butter and cheese. Others worked at various trades in the workshops. No task was too lowly for them. Most of the monasteries followed the rules laid down by St. Benedict, a monk who was head of a monastery in Italy in the sixth century, and one of the sayings of the good St. Benedict was: "Idleness is an enemy of the soul. To labor is to pray."

The monks also believed in learning, and for centuries they had within their monastery walls the only schools in existence. The churchmen were about the only people who could read and write; even most nobles and kings could not write their names. Only those who had gone to the monasteries and learned from the monks knew their letters. The monastery schools were attended by young nobles who wished to master the art of reading and writing in Latin, and by boys who wished to study to become priests.

There were homes of the same kind, called convents, for women, who wished to become nuns. Giving up the beautiful garments of the day, the nuns wore a white undergarment, a black gown and veil, and a white wimple around the face and neck. They employed themselves mainly with spinning and weaving and fine needlecraft. Most of the richly embroidered altar pieces and banners used in the churches were the work of their skillful fingers. The good sisters had schools, too, where the daughters of nobles could learn the fine art of embroidery from the nuns.

Attached to many of the monasteries were hospitals where the monks cared for the sick. Every monastery also had monks appointed to care for the needy, to give them food and clothing. So it became the custom for friendless people who were in trouble to seek the nearest monastery or convent for help. Every day at a certain hour the poor came to the gates and the monks gave them bread and wine. Thus they cared for the poor and suffering.

Monasteries served still another purpose. Although there was not much traveling in early medieval days, some men did travel; and when they did, they could not find places where they could be accommodated for the night or get their meals, as there were few inns. So the monasteries opened their gates to wayfarers and built guest houses for them, and certain of the monks were appointed to serve them. Many a weary, footsore traveler found rest and refreshment in the monasteries and was cared for by the good brothers.

The medieval world owed much to the devout dwellers in

the monasteries. The monastery was the center of the life of its neighborhood. There the ignorant were taught, the helpless protected, the poor sheltered, the hungry fed, the sick cared for. When trouble of any kind came to anyone it was to the monastery that he turned for advice and help. Life within the monastery walls was a peaceful, well-ordered existence, where, sheltered from the turmoil of the world, the monks lived lives of quiet industry, self-sacrifice, and devotion to duty according to the Christian ideal.

As the centuries rolled by many of the monasteries became rich, for many men made them presents, because they hoped in this way to win forgiveness for their wrongdoing. Then in some of the monasteries changes crept in. Some men became monks because they wanted a comfortable place to live; and idleness, luxury, and other evils grew up. But for many centuries the monasteries did a much-needed work and were one of the great civilizing forces of the Middle Ages.

XII

Scribes

ALL through the early Middle Ages the only books in existence were those produced by the monks. These were called manuscripts, which means written by hand, for in those days people did not know how to print with type and every book was carefully and painstakingly written by the scribes, as the monks who made books were called. All day long, except when they were chanting the masses, certain of the monks were in their little stone-walled, stone-floored alcoves around the cloister copying huge volumes with infinite patience. In some of the monasteries there was a large writing room, called a scriptorium, where all the monks who were skillful penmen or illuminators worked together writing books.

There were very strict rules in the scriptorium. No one except the scribes and the head of the monastery was allowed to enter it. One of the monks supervised the work. He had to provide all the necessary materials and give out the work to the others. No one was allowed to speak, so the scribes used sign language to communicate with one another and to make known their wants. If one needed a book he made the motion of turning over the leaves. If it was a book of prayers he wanted, he would make the sign of the cross. If he wanted a book by a pagan author he would scratch his ears like a dog.

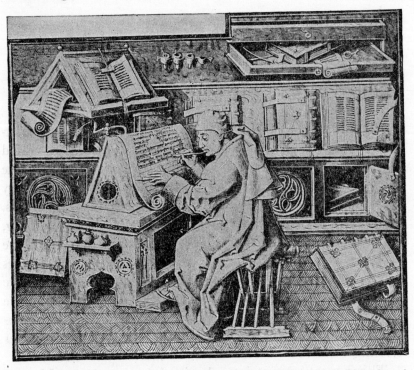

A medieval scribe at work on his manuscript. (From *The Miracles of Our Lady,* a fifteenth-century book.)

Books in medieval days were not made of paper. They were written on vellum, which was made from calf's skin, or parchment, made from sheep's skin, which the monks prepared themselves. First the hide was soaked in lime water to remove the hair. Then it was washed thoroughly and stretched on a frame to dry. Then it was rubbed with pumice stone until it was thin and smooth. At last, after much careful work, there was a beautiful, creamy piece of vellum or parchment which the scribe cut into pieces of the right size for his book. Down each side of the page broad margins were marked off; holes were pricked at intervals with a sharp awl and lines drawn across the page from hole to hole with a metal stylus as a guide for the writing; spaces were left for illuminations.

With his ruled leaves before him, and all things necessary for his work—ink made from soot mixed with gum and acid, pens made from goose quills or reeds, ruler, and weights to hold down the pages—the scribe began the work of writing, slowly forming the large, square, curious-looking Gothic letters in use at the time. The letters were so carefully made that they were almost as regular as if they had been printed.

The scribes delighted in ornamenting the initial letter of a chapter or a page with fine gold or rich colors—crimson, and deep blue, and green—and they scattered here and there throughout the text beautiful little colored pictures of angels and saints or scenes from everyday life. In some books the borders around each page were elaborately ornamented with garlands and vines, and often, tucked away almost out of sight in the flowery margins, were quaint little animals—butterflies and bees, scarlet ladybugs and pale green dragonflies with wings like rainbows, fuzzy caterpillars, and little snails in their curled shells. How lovely the pages were with their wonderful initial letters, their beautiful illuminations, glittering with gold and colors like little mosaics, and their margins garlanded with flowers!

A famous monk whose beautiful illuminations have come down to us was Fra Giovanni, of the monastery of San Marco in Florence. He was most saintly in his ways and so good and gentle that his fellow monks called him Fra Angelico, which means angel-like brother, and that is the name by which he has been known to the world ever since. He covered the pages of his manuscripts with beautiful little miniatures. He loved to paint angels, pure and gentle, angels blowing trumpets, angels with cymbals, angels singing praises to God, with halos about their heads and delicately tinted wings. Sometimes he made a diptych, or a triptych, which are paintings made on two or three panels of wood hinged together. These were used to adorn the altar of the monastery church. He also painted lovely pictures of scenes from the Bible on the bare walls of the monastery, so that the monks might have these scenes from the holy book to look at and think about.

Day after day, month after month, the patient monk in the dimly lighted scriptorium, or in his little alcove, bent over his sheets of parchment or vellum, forming each letter perfectly, and his book grew in beauty. At last it was finished. The scribe took such a delight in the pages he had made, he felt sure the dear Lord himself could not but be pleased with his work, so he would often add a little prayer at the end of the book.

138

Deus in adiutorium
meum intende
Domine ad adiu
uandum me festina
Gloria patri et filio et spiritui
sancto
Sicut erat in principio et nunc
et semper: et in secula seculorum.
Amen. Hymnus.
Memento salutis auctor q
nostri quondam corporis ex illiba
ta Virgine nascendo formam su
pseris
Maria mater gratie mater mi
sericordie tu nos ab hoste protege
et hora mortis suscipe
Gloria tibi domine qui natus

A page from a medieval manuscript.

Here is one of these prayers:

I, Brother Stephen, of the Abbey of St. Martin de Bouchase, made this book; and for every initial letter and picture and border of flowers that I have herein wrought, I pray the Lord God to have compassion upon some one of my grievous sins.

Here is a prayer from a book in a monastery library:

O, Lord, send the blessing of Thy holy spirit upon these books, that, cleansing them of all earthly things, they may mercifully enlighten our hearts and give us a true understanding, and grant that by their teaching they may brightly preserve and make full abundance of good works according to Thy will.

It was often with a sense of relief that a monk finished his long task. One tired worker added a little note at the end of his manuscript: "He who does not know how to write imagines that it is no labor, but though only three fingers hold the pen the whole body grows weary." Another one wrote: "I pray you good readers who may use this book do not forget him who copied it. It was a poor brother, named Louis, who, while he copied the volume, endured the cold and was obliged to finish in the night what he could not write by day." Still another one expressed his feelings thus: "You do not know what it is to write. It hurts your back, it obscures your eyes, it cramps your sides and your stomach."

When all the pages were finished, they were usually bound in leather and made beautiful with heavy, carved silver corners and huge clasps. Some books were covered with velvet, some with ivory, delicately carved. Some covers were of beaten gold, exquisitely wrought, and set with pearls and other jewels.

The monks copied Bibles, hymns and prayers, the lives of the saints, as well as the writings of the Greeks and Romans and other ancient peoples, preserving in this way the stories and histories that would otherwise have been lost to the world. Almost every monastery kept a chronicle—or record of important events—year by year. So the monks became the historians of their day, and it is from their writings that we derive a great deal of our knowledge of the life, customs, and events of medieval times.

Among the most popular books was one called a book of hours, which had a text from the Bible for each hour of the day and a calendar showing all the feast days of the church during the year. Such books were gifts fit for a queen or a king. King Louis XII of France gave a beautiful one as a wedding gift to Lady Anne of Bretagne.

The scribes did a great service to civilization, for through their work many valuable books are preserved to us today that otherwise might have been lost to the world. Many of these beautiful books are still kept in museums and libraries, both in Europe and in this country, and are regarded as their choicest treasures.

XIII

Little Brothers of the Poor

BESIDES the monks there were other holy men, called friars, who did a great work in medieval days. Instead of retiring to quiet monasteries, as the monks did, they went out into the world to hunt out the needy and care for the sick. With self-sacrificing zeal these cowled figures wandered penniless and barefoot from place to place. Having parted with all their worldly goods, they lived on whatever people gave them, and preached the gospel to any who would listen to them. They brought comfort and help to thousands whom the priests and monks did not reach. There were several orders —gray friars, white friars, black friars—the color of their gowns marking the order to which they belonged.

St. Francis, the founder of the Franciscan order, was the most beloved of all the friars. He was born in Assisi, a little walled town built on a hillside in central Italy. He was the son of a wealthy cloth merchant, and when he was a young man he led a gay, carefree life and spent his father's money freely.

Through the narrow, winding streets of Assisi young Francis Bernardone went forth every evening with a company of light-hearted gallants dressed in doublets of velvet

142

and long hose of silk, scarlet and purple or orange and magenta and green. They sang love songs and frolicked through the streets of the little town long after sober citizens were in bed. Thus, with a gay round of fetes and festivals, revels, and adventures, the early life of St. Francis was spent.

In spite of all his gayety, however, Francis felt deep pity for the misery of the poor. The contrast between their lives and his own life of luxury affected him deeply. And often he gave all the money in his well-filled purse to poor beggars whom he met. Once when he was in Rome he noticed a beggar who, sitting near a church, stretched out his thin hand and looked wistfully into people's faces. No one seemed to pay any attention to him. Francis wondered what it would be like to sit all day from morning till night, begging for one's daily bread. Suddenly he led the astonished man to a deserted corner, poured silver and gold into his hands, and proposed changing clothes with him. Quickly he pulled off his own rich cloak and gave it to the man, and then Francis, dressed in the beggar's tattered garments, sat all day at the door of St. Peter's Church.

After a long, serious illness, when he was about twenty years old, Francis realized more than ever before the emptiness of the life he had been leading and decided to give it up. His father and his friends tried in vain to make him change his mind. When finally his father threatened to disinherit him, Francis cheerfully agreed to surrender his inheritance. He stripped off his costly doublet and hose, his white linen shirt and fine undergarments, and in exchange for them he took a coarse brown gown. He picked up a piece of mortar and chalked a cross on the front of it. For a girdle he took a piece of rope that happened to be lying on the ground nearby.

Then, bareheaded and barefoot, Francis wandered from town to town, caring for the sick, begging from the rich and giving to the poor, living on what was given him to eat from day to day, and teaching everyone about the goodness of God. His aim was to live as nearly as possible as Christ had lived on earth, devoting his life to the loving service of others. And so beloved was St. Francis that when a village heard of his approach, the whole population turned out in joyful procession to meet him. "He is our brother," they said, "and a friend of all the world."

Other young men decided to strip themselves of their worldly possessions and follow the example of St. Francis. Thus the order of the Franciscan friars came into existence. The new society spread rapidly through Europe. Within ten years there were five thousand Little Brothers of the Poor, as they were sometimes called. They were pledged not to possess house or land, but to live in the utmost simplicity and give themselves wholly to the service of God by working among the poor and needy.

St. Francis loved not only men, women, and children; his heart overflowed with love for all living creatures. Some beautiful old stories have come down to us telling of the love of St. Francis for animals. Those who knew him told the stories to their children and grandchildren, until there gathered about his name many tender little tales and legends,

144

St. Francis preaching to the birds. (From a painting by Giotto.)

some true and some probably what people loved to think might have been true.

One old writer tells the following story: One day St. Francis was walking with one of his brothers. As they came to a little town St. Francis lifted his eyes and beheld some trees near by in which were a flock of little birds, and more of them in a field. And he said to his companion, "Tarry here for me upon the way, and I will go to preach unto my sisters, the birds." And he went into the field and began to preach to the birds that were on the ground; immediately those that were in the trees flew down to him, and they all remained still and quiet together.

The sermon that St. Francis preached to the birds was somewhat after this fashion: "My little sisters, the birds, much are ye beholden unto God, your Creator, and always ought ye to praise Him, for He hath given you liberty to fly about everywhere, and God feedeth you and giveth you streams and fountains for your drink, mountains and valleys for your refuge, and the high trees whereon to make your nests; wherefore your Creator loveth you much, seeing that He hath bestowed on you so many benefits."

The story declares that while St. Francis spoke the birds arched their necks and spread their wings, and by their acts showed that the holy father gave them great joy. St. Francis rejoiced with them and was glad.

At last, having ended his preaching, St. Francis made the sign of the cross over the birds and gave them leave to go away. And all soared high up into the air singing most sweetly and then divided into four parts after the fashion of
146

the cross that St. Francis had made over them. And one part flew toward the east, and another toward the west, and a third toward the north, and the fourth toward the south, each flock by their wondrous songs betokening that, even as St. Francis had preached to them and they had divided singing to the four quarters of the earth, so the preaching of Christ's word through St. Francis would be borne all over the world.

Another story tells about St. Francis and a wolf. About fifteen miles north of Assisi is the little village of Gubbio. One day St. Francis came to the village and found the inhabitants huddled up in the market place, afraid to stir out into the fields because there was a terrible wolf out there, the largest and fiercest ever known, who devoured not only animals but people.

St. Francis went forth unafraid, putting his trust in God. The wolf came leaping toward him with its great jaws wide open, but St. Francis made the sign of the cross and spoke to him softly, saying, "Come hither, Brother Wolf. I command that thou do no harm to me nor to anyone." And the terrible wolf closed his jaws and gently as a lamb came and lay down at the feet of St. Francis.

Then St. Francis spoke to him thus: "Brother Wolf, much harm hast thou wrought in these parts and done grievous ill, slaying the creatures of God, and all cry out against thee. But I would fain make peace between thee and them so that they may forgive thee for thy past offenses."

At these words the wolf by the movements of his body and his tail and eyes gave sign that he understood what St. Fran-

147

cis was saying. Then spake St. Francis again: "Brother Wolf, I will see to it that the folk of this place give thee food always so long as thou shalt live, so that thou suffer not from hunger any more, for I wot well that through hunger hast thou wrought all this ill. But since I win for thee this grace, I will that thou promise me to do no hurt to any one, man or beast. Dost promise me this?"

The wolf gave clear token by the nodding of his head that he promised. Then St. Francis stretched forth his hand to take the pledge of his troth, and the wolf lifted up his right paw and laid it gently in the hand of St. Francis. Then said St. Francis, "Brother Wolf, I bid thee now come with me." And the wolf, obedient, set forth with him in fashion gentle as a lamb.

As the news spread through the village, all the people—menfolk and womenfolk, great and small, young and old—gathered together in the market place to see the wolf with St. Francis.

And St. Francis said: "Give ear, my brothers. Brother Wolf, who standeth before you, hath promised me to make peace with you and to offend no one in any way. Do ye promise him to give him every day whatever he needs, and I am sure that he will keep this pact of peace right steadfastly."

Then promised all the folk to give the wolf food: Then said St. Francis to the wolf before them all: "And thou, Brother Wolf, dost thou make promise to keep firm this pact of peace that thou offend not man, nor beast, nor any creature?" And the wolf knelt down and bowed his head and with gentle
148

movements of his body, tail, and eyes gave sign, as best he could, that he would keep the pact. This wrought such great joy and marvel in all the people that they began to lift up their voices, praising God who had sent St. Francis to them to set them free from the jaws of the cruel beast.

Thereafter this same wolf lived in Gubbio and went like a tame beast in and out of the houses and from door to door without doing hurt to anyone, and was carefully nourished by all the people.

Almost the last thing we know about St. Francis is the beautiful Canticle of the Sun, a hymn of gratitude which came to him one day shortly before he died:

O most high, almighty, good Lord God, to Thee belong praise, glory, honor, and all blessing!

Praised be my Lord God with all His creatures, and especially our brother the sun, who brings us the day and who brings us the light; fair is he and shining with a very great splendor. O Lord he signifies to us Thee!

Praised be my Lord for our sister the moon, and for the stars, the which He hath set clear and lovely in the heaven.

Praised be my Lord for our brother, the wind, and for air and cloud, calms, and all weather, by the which Thou upholdest in life all creatures.

Praised be my Lord for our sister water, who is very serviceable unto us, and humble, and precious, and clean.

149

Praised be my Lord for our brother fire, through whom Thou givest us light in the darkness; and he is bright and pleasant, and very mighty, and strong.

Praised be my Lord for our mother the earth, the which doth sustain us and keep us, and bringeth forth divers fruits, and flowers of many colors, and grass.

Praised be my Lord for all those who pardon one another for His love's sake, and who endure weakness and tribulation; blessed are they who peaceably shall endure for Thou, O most Highest, shalt give them a crown.

*   *   *

Praise ye, and bless ye the Lord, and give thanks unto Him, and serve Him with great humility.

XIV

God Wills It!

RELIGION led many people to make long journeys as pilgrims during the Middle Ages. From quite early times devout Christians of Europe had made pilgrimages to Palestine, called the Holy Land, to the hallowed scenes of Christ's life in Jerusalem. Such a pilgrimage, it was believed, showed penitence for anything wrong that a person had done and would win God's forgiveness. Sometimes it was an act of thanksgiving for some good fortune or for some harm or bodily ill escaped. Clad in a rough gown, with bare feet and a staff in his hand, a pilgrim would set out, begging food and shelter on the road, as he made his way to the Holy City. There he knelt and prayed and felt that he was blessed for his act of devotion.

In the seventh century Palestine was conquered by the Arabs. Although they were followers of Mohammed they allowed the Christian pilgrims to visit Jerusalem without being disturbed. But in the eleventh century the Turks, a much more barbarous people than the Arabs, captured Jerusalem and they often treated the Christian pilgrims cruelly. Pilgrims who returned to Europe from the Holy Land told dreadful tales of hardship and suffering. This aroused a storm of indignation among the people of Europe.

In 1095 Pope Urban II called a great meeting at Clermont, France. Clergy and nobles flocked there from all over Europe. On a widespreading plain the Pope addressed the assembled multitude in a powerful sermon. "A race wholly alienated from God," said he, "has violently invaded the lands of the Christians and either destroyed the churches of God or appropriated them for their own religion." He told them of the hard fate of the pilgrims to Jerusalem. "They have dragged away captives into far-distant countries, and yoking them with thongs, have compelled them to plow the land like oxen and to undergo other toils befitting beasts rather than men. Our brethren are flogged with whips, urged with goads, and subjected to innumerable sufferings," he said.

Then the Pope appealed to the faith and courage of the proud knights and urged them to begin a war to wrest the Holy Land from the infidels. "On whom is the labor of avenging these wrongs of recovering this territory incumbent, if not on you?" he asked.

"Christ Himself will be your leader," the Pope continued, "when, like the Israelites of old, you fight for Jerusalem. Every spot there is hallowed by the words Christ spake, by the miracles He performed. Let none of your possessions detain you, nor solicitude for your family affairs. Enter upon the road to the Holy Land and wrest it from the wicked race and subject it to yourselves."

As the venerable Pope spoke, many of his hearers were

so deeply affected by his eloquence that they wept, and cries of "Deus vult! Deus vult!" [God wills it] burst from the throng, carried away by his words.

Lifting his hand to command silence, the Pope replied, "It is, in truth, the will of God. Let these words be your battle cry and this be your guide," holding aloft a cross. "Christ's cross is indeed the symbol of your salvation. Wear it, a red cross on breast or shoulder, as a symbol of your zeal in the service of Christ."

From all sides the knights pressed forward to have the red cross placed upon their breasts. To those who took the cross the name crusader was given from the Latin word *crux,* which means cross.

This religious excitement spread over all Europe. Preachers everywhere took up the cry, "God wills it!" and urged the people to "take the cross" and start for the Holy Land. Among the pilgrims who had been to the Holy Land was Peter, a monk who had become a hermit. He had been horrified to find that Christians were being persecuted, and he thought he heard the voice of God, saying, "Rise, Peter, go forth to make known the tribulations of My people; the hour is come for the recovery of the holy places."

Peter returned to Europe, inspired with the idea of rousing the Christians to go to the rescue of the pilgrims in the East. Clad in a long coarse robe, tied about the waist with a rope, riding on a donkey and carrying a large crucifix, for two years he traveled through France, Italy, and Germany, preaching in the market places, or wherever he could get an audience together, making fervent appeals to

153

the people to join in the holy war to rescue the Holy Sepulcher. His cheeks were hollow, and he was worn with suffering; and wherever he went rich and poor, old and young, fastened the red cross on their cloaks, resolved to set off for the Holy Land.

The following spring a motley crowd of peasants, workmen, even women and children, set out for distant Palestine, led by Peter the Hermit, and a poor knight called Walter the Penniless. Without proper provisions or arms, they started out on a journey of two thousand miles, ignorant of the distance, of the route, and of the dangers and hardships before them. Many of them perished on the way from sickness or starvation; others were captured and sold as slaves. Some of them, however, ragged and half-starved, but inspired by a great faith, did succeed in reaching Palestine.

When, at last, the white walls of the Holy City came in sight they fell upon their knees and, with tears and prayers of thanksgiving, kissed the sacred soil. Then, with Peter the Hermit at their head, they marched barefoot in a procession around the walls. Afterward, an old account tells us, "they went rejoicing, nay, from excess of joy, weeping, to the tomb of our Savior to adore and give thanks," and the sobs of the weeping multitude, it is said, "sounded, at a distance, like the rustling leaves of a mighty forest, or the coming in of the ocean tide."

Meanwhile the nobles were making ready for an expedition, and the first properly organized and equipped crusading army set out later in the same year. They fought

Crusaders on their way to Jerusalem. (From *The Grand Voyage de Hierusalem*, printed in 1522.)

the Turks with such success that they captured Jerusalem and set up a Christian kingdom there. So, in 1099, the Holy City was once more in the hands of the Christians. The Crusaders had fulfilled their vow to wrest the Holy Sepulcher from the infidel, and the First Crusade came to an end.

For years after the Crusaders had taken Jerusalem all went well. Many Christians settled there, and a Christian government was set up. There was peace between the Turks and the Christians, and pilgrims were once more able to visit the Holy Sepulcher in safety.

About fifty years after the First Crusade, Jerusalem was attacked by strong Turkish forces, the Christians in the Holy Land appealed for help, and soon bands of Crusaders set out once more. But the Second Crusade had an unhappy ending. Only a few thousand of those who set out escaped from the Turks, who set upon them before they reached Jerusalem. Not many years after the Second Crusade, the Mohammedans found a great leader in the sultan Saladin, as renowned for his noble virtues as he was for his zeal for the Mohammedan faith. In 1187 Saladin succeeded in getting Jerusalem back from the Christians.

When news of the loss of the Holy City reached Europe it again stirred up religious zeal, and once more thousands sewed the red cross on their garments and set out on that perilous journey to the Holy Land. Three of the most powerful rulers in Europe led their armies during this crusade: Frederick Barbarossa of Germany, Philip of France, and Richard I of England, so famed for his courage that men called him the Lionhearted.

156

God Wills It!

When the Crusaders reached Palestine they found the Christians laying siege to Acre, a seaport near Jerusalem. The siege dragged on for a year, but at length Acre was captured, largely through the efforts of King Richard, who was one of the best warriors of his day. So, although Jerusalem was yet to be taken, the Christians were in possession of the coast of Palestine.

Soon after this Richard received news that his brother John had been plotting to seize the throne of England and make himself king, so he made a truce with Saladin and started home. On his way he was shipwrecked and had to go through the territory of an enemy, Duke Leopold of Austria. He knew that the journey would be dangerous, so he disguised himself as a pilgrim; but it is said that he carelessly left a jeweled ring on his finger when he stopped at an inn. By this he was recognized, and he was seized and cast into a dungeon. A whole year elapsed, and none of the people in England had any idea where their king was imprisoned.

A pretty story is told as to how Richard was discovered by means of a song. The favorite minstrel of the king was one Blondel de Nesle. He resolved to try to find his beloved master. With his lyre under his arm, he wandered over Europe searching everywhere, listening to all the gossip of people in towns and at inns, but nowhere did he get news of Richard. At length fate directed him to the village where the king was imprisoned. He heard from some of the inhabitants that a noble captive was being held in a certain castle. Suspecting that it was Richard, Blondel stationed himself beneath a window of the castle, began to play his lyre, and sang the first verse of a little song Richard and he had composed together:

> *Your beauty, lady fair,*
> *None views without delight;*
> *But still so cold an air*
> *No passion can excite;*
> *This yet I patient see*
> *While all are shunned like me.*

As the minstrel paused, suddenly he heard from within the dungeon the clear voice of a singer, who took up the song and finished it:

> *No nymph my heart can wound*
> *If favor she divide;*
> *And smiles on all around*
> *Unwilling to decide;*
> *I'd rather hatred bear*
> *Than love with others share.*

Overjoyed at hearing once more the well-known voice, Blondel hastened back to tell the barons the good news. They paid a heavy ransom, and Richard was released.

There were several later Crusades. In fact, off and on for two hundred years kings and nobles continued to lead expeditions to the East. But the later Crusades were of little importance, and before the end of the thirteenth century
158

the old crusading spirit died out and the Crusades came to an end.

The Crusaders were unsuccessful in doing what they set out to do. After two hundred years of conflict the Holy Land still remained in the hands of the Mohammedans. Nevertheless, the Crusades did much for the people of Europe. They brought them in contact with the rich and splendid civilizations of the East, and the Crusaders brought back to Europe with them many new ideas which profoundly affected life in Europe in later centuries. Of the great influence of the Crusades upon medieval civilization we shall have more to tell later on in the book.

XV

Pilgrimages

ALTHOUGH Jerusalem was the great place for pilgrimages, there were other shrines nearer home for those who were unable to undertake such a long, perilous journey, and many pilgrims visited the graves of martyrs and saints in various parts of Europe.

While a very holy man was alive people almost worshiped him, and when he died they sent to the Pope the story of his life, and the Pope, after he had examined into the record, if he found it worthy, declared the holy man a saint. Hundreds of men and women were made saints in this way. It was believed that the blessed saints offered their prayers in heaven for men. Hence people prayed to the saints and asked them to intercede with God for them. The places where they were buried became sacred shrines, and many people visited them and humbly begged to be forgiven for any wrongs they had done or to be cured of their bodily ills.

In England the most famous shrine was the tomb of Thomas à Becket in the cathedral at Canterbury. In the early part of the reign of Henry II his chief adviser was Thomas à Becket. Henry showered riches and favors upon him, and in return Thomas à Becket served his king well.

160

For years the king and his chancellor were the best of friends. Then Henry made Becket Archbishop of Canter-

The martyrdom of Thomas à Becket. (From a thirteenth-century manuscript.)

bury, which was the highest position in the English church, thinking that thus he could check the authority of the

161

church. This proved to be a mistake, for as soon as Becket became archbishop he was a changed man. He renounced all his luxury and put his duty to the church higher than his duty to his king.

The change in Becket surprised and offended Henry, who saw that he could no longer depend on Becket's doing as he wished him to do. One day, in the presence of some nobles, Henry, in a fit of anger, exclaimed, "What a pack of cowards I have about me that no one will rid me of this troublesome, low-born priest!"

Then four knights, without Henry's knowledge, secretly made their way to Canterbury. When the knights arrived there the terrified monks persuaded the archbishop to go to the cathedral for safety. Fully armed, the knights rushed into the cathedral, crying, "Where is the traitor?"

Becket came down the steps of the choir, majestic in his bishop's robes. "Behold me," he replied. "No traitor, but a priest of the most high God."

The knights threatened him, but Becket was fearless. "If all the swords in England were now at my head," he said, "I would not yield."

Then, in their madness, the knights fell upon Becket and struck him down at the foot of the altar.

To kill anyone within the sacred precincts of the church was an unspeakable crime, and the news of Becket's death filled all Europe with horror. The people feared that the curse of God would fall on a land where such a terrible thing had been done. Becket became a holy martyr of the church, and a magnificent shrine was built for him in the

162

cathedral where he had lost his life. No one was more horrified than Henry when he heard the dreadful news. Filled with remorse at the result of his hasty words, he walked as a humble pilgrim with bare and bleeding feet along the rough road to Canterbury and, kneeling at the dead archbishop's tomb, did penance for his sin.

Miller   Clerk of Oxford

Some Canterbury pilgrims. (From the Ellesmere manuscript.)

After that it was a frequent sight in the spring of the year to see bands of pilgrims making their way to Canterbury to the martyr's shrine. In the course of time these pilgrimages came to be looked upon as outings. There was always a sense of adventure in a journey to a new place in medieval times, and it gave people a chance to see the world.

163

The pilgrims often passed the time pleasantly on the way by exchanging stories of their experiences, and sometimes they related strange tales they had heard in distant lands. They stopped at inns en route, for the bad roads of the time made traveling slow, and most people accomplished not more than twenty miles a day.

Squire   Prioress

Some Canterbury pilgrims. (From the Ellesmere manuscript.)

Chaucer, the great English poet of the fourteenth century, tells us in his *Canterbury Tales* about a little company of pilgrims that met at the Tabard Inn, at Southwark, not far from London. Harry Baily, the jolly host of the inn, proposed that each member of the company should tell two tales on the way to Canterbury and two on the return

164

journey, and whoever told the best tale was to have supper at the expense of the rest. In the prologue to the tales Chaucer describes the pilgrims and gives us a very good picture of fourteenth-century life, for the pilgrims were drawn from all classes of the society of his day.

Leading the pilgrims was a knight.

> *... a worthy man,*
> *That fro the tyme that he first bigan*
> *To riden out, he loved chyvalrye*
> *Trouthe, and honour, fredom and courteisye.*
>
> *And though that he was worthy, he was wys,*
> *And of his port as meke as is a mayde.*
> *He never yet no villeinye ne sayde*
> *In al his lyf, unto no maner wight.*
> *He was a verray parfit, gentil knyght.*

With the knight was his son, a young squire

> *With lokkes curled as they were leyd in presse,*
> *Of twenty yeer of age he was, I gesse.*
> *Embroidered was he as it were a mede*
> *Al ful of freshe flowres, whyte and rede.*
> *Synging he was or fluting al the day.*
> *He was as fressh as is the month of May.*

With them was their servant, a yeoman, "clad in cote and hood of grene," with a sheaf of arrows in his belt and in his hand a mighty bow.

The church was represented by a little nun with her gracefully pleated wimple and her black cloak over a white tunic.

> *She was so charitable and so pitious*
> *She wolde wepe, if that she sawe a mous*
> *Caught in a trappe.*

Then came a monk, a striking figure:

> *His heed was balled, that shoon as any glas,*
> *And eke his face, as he had been anoint.*
> *He was a lord, ful fat and in good poynt.*

Next the monk rode a friar, and with him rode a poor parish priest.

> *Christes lore and His apostles twelve*
> *He taughte, but first he folwed it hymselve.*

Learning was there in the person of the hollow-cheeked student of Oxford with his threadbare cloak. The humbler trades and occupations were represented by a cook, a poor plowman, and a miller; and the guildsmen by

> *An haberdasher and a carpenter,*
> *A webbe, a dyere, and a tapycer,*
> *And they were clothed alle in a lyveree*
> *Of a solemne and greet fraternitee.*

166

Perhaps you may enjoy reading the whole prologue to the poem, which describes all the pilgrims. Some of the words may look strange to you, and the old spelling sometimes makes them difficult to understand; but with a little help at first you will soon get used to the old English.

Towns and Town Life

XVI

Merchants and Craftsmen

IN THE early part of the Middle Ages there were almost no towns in western Europe. During the Dark Ages, when the barbarians were swarming over Europe, many of the towns that had grown up under Roman rule fell into ruins, and most of the people lived in the country in the castles of the feudal lords. But gradually little settlements began to grow up under the sheltering protection of the castles, or near a monastery, or at some place like the crossing of two roads, or on a river, where trade could be carried on.

The towns in medieval days were very different from those of today. Most of them were surrounded by high stone walls and moats, for protection, just as the castles were. They could be entered only through big gateways, and watchmen were always on guard to give the alarm at the approach of an enemy. At nightfall the gates were swung shut, and no one could enter the town except by special permission.

Towns were generally built around a large open square. On one side was the town hall, usually a splendid Gothic building with a high belfry, where the business of the town was carried on. On another side was the church, or perhaps a cathedral, which was a bishop's church. Around the square clustered the houses of the townsfolk. The narrow and winding streets were often picturesque, with their rows of high-peaked houses, with their fronts quaintly carved and decorated and their upper stories sometimes jutting

A street in a medieval town.

out so far that neighbors could almost shake hands across the street from their upstairs windows. Most of the streets were unpaved, and as there were no sewers the rain water often stood in them in deep puddles or flowed through them in muddy streams.

At eight or nine o'clock at night, when the big bell in the town hall rang out the curfew (which comes from the

French words *couvre feu,* meaning cover fire) the townspeople were compelled to cover their fires with ashes and
put out their lights. This was a wise rule, as most of the
houses were built of wood and were so close together that if

A street scene during a fair. In the middle are a townsman and his wife
returning home after making their purchases. Behind them are a knight
and his attendant on horseback. At the right is the shop of a cloth
merchant and next to it an inn. At the left is a money-changer and a
beggar.

a fire broke out it was likely to spread through the whole
town. The streets were unlighted at night, and anyone who
went out after nightfall had to carry a lighted torch which
had been dipped in pitch. Very likely he would have to give

173

an account of himself to the night watch, who were citizens that took turns guarding the town.

Markets were held in the town square one or two days each week. Stalls were set up, and to the town the near-by

A shoemaker's shop. (From a sixteenth-century woodcut.)

manors sent their surplus to be disposed of. Once or twice a year a town might hold a fair, to which foreign-looking merchants came from distant places bringing bales of fine woolen cloth on the backs of pack horses, or silks, or carpets, and other things not usually on sale in the little shops of

174

the town or at the weekly markets in the market place.
During fair time the town presented a busy scene. In the
square, or in some field just outside the town, would spring
up rows of wooden booths and stalls. All kinds of strolling

A hatter and his apprentices. (From a sixteenth-century woodcut.)

players and showmen flocked to the fairs. Tumblers and
minstrels gathered little knots of people about them. There
were men with performing bears, and trained horses, and
acrobats exhibiting their tricks. Peddlers and hawkers
loudly called their wares, and throngs of customers and

175

pleasure seekers crowded up to the booths to buy and to enjoy the sights. Every road and lane leading to the town was filled with a throng of travelers on beasts or afoot, as people came to the fair from near and far. For two or three

An armorer. (From a sixteenth-century woodcut.)

weeks the hubbub might continue. Then the merchants would pack up their unsold wares, take down their tents, and make their way to another fair; the amusement makers would disappear to wander to another place; and the little town would settle down once more to its quiet, everyday life.

176

Let us imagine that we are taking a walk through the winding streets of a medieval town. The shops of many craftsmen line the narrow sidewalks. They are like little open booths, where the workmen are busy at their work and

Smiths. (From a sixteenth-century woodcut.)

their wares are offered for sale, for the making and selling is done on the first floor of the workman's home, and goods are sold directly from the maker to the user. Many gay signs swing out over the shop doors, on which are painted devices to suggest the business of the shop owner—a golden fleece

177

for the wool merchant, a unicorn for a goldsmith, and so on. As so few people could read, the shopkeepers took this means of showing the passer-by what was sold within.

The men engaged in the same craft usually lived side by side on the same street or in the same part of a town. There was a street of armorers, a street of butchers, a street of workers in wool, and so on. In London the iron workers lived in Ironmongers' Lane, the bakers in Bread Street, the tailors in Threadneedle Street, the tanners in Tanners' Row, the candlemakers in Candlewick Street, and the goldsmiths in Goldsmiths' Lane. Even today it is possible to walk along Bread Street, Milk Street, and Threadneedle Street in London.

Often in those days a man came to be known by the name of his trade. A worker in metals was called a smith, and he might come to be known in the town as John, the smith. A pottery worker might be known as James, the potter. In time such men came to be called John Smith and James Potter. Many families today have names that have come from the trades of the Middle Ages. I can think of several: Carpenter, Miller, Baker, Weaver, Shoemaker; perhaps you can think of others.

Let us stop for a moment and look into a goldsmith's shop. We can see several young boys at work with simple tools. They are apprentices who are learning their trade from the goldsmith. The master of the shop is moving about, waiting on customers, showing the apprentices how to do their tasks, and doing some of the hardest parts of the work himself. Gold is being melted and refined and beaten into various

178

shapes with little hammers, and in many things precious jewels are being set. Everything is done in the little shop where the goods are sold, and each worker makes the whole thing, taking the raw material and, with a few simple tools, making it into the finished product.

A goldsmith's shop in Paris about 1500. (From an engraving made by the goldsmith himself.)

So it was in all the trades. The armorer made a helmet, carrying through every part of the work from the first shaping of the steel to the attaching of the plume at the top; the shoemaker selected the leather and did every part of the

179

making of boots and shoes. How different that way of doing things is from our present method, where things are manufactured in factories by many workmen, each one doing a small part of the work at a machine, and then the finished product is passed through the wholesale houses on to the retail seller before it reaches us.

At first the towns had little trade, producing only what their own inhabitants needed. It was difficult to send goods from place to place. Roads were poor and were infested with robbers, and on the water there was the danger of shipwreck and attacks by pirates. But from the eleventh century on the demand for greater luxuries called for skilled workers of all sorts and led to a great development of the various trades. Armorers were needed to make the armor of the nobles, goldsmiths made jewelry for the lords and ladies, the building of churches and monasteries called for masons, stonecutters, carpenters, and glass workers, as well as artistic iron work and wood carving. The magnificent dress of the day made work for many men skilled in weaving and dyeing, and the richly embroidered altar cloths and vestments of the church made work for women skilled with the needle.

XVII

In the Days of the Guilds

THE merchants of a town soon found that by acting together they could accomplish much that no one of them could do alone. So they began banding together in associations, called guilds. Their object was to control the trade of the town. A guild usually made it unlawful for a stranger to come into the town and sell goods, except under the regulations of the guild. A weaver from another town, for instance, could not bring in his cloth and offer it for sale. Neither could a baker, nor a tailor, nor any other tradesman from another place carry on business in the town. Thus the business of the town was kept for its own guild members.

After a while the craftsmen in the towns followed the example of the merchants and formed various guilds according to the kind of work they did. The movement spread rapidly, and in time there were guilds of carpenters, weavers, millers, butchers, bakers, grocers, tailors, goldsmiths, armorers, masons, shoemakers—in fact, practically every kind of work had its guild, and no one was allowed to engage in a craft unless he was a member of a guild. Each guild chose its officers and levied dues to pay its expenses.

The guilds stood for just weights and measures and

181

honesty in all business transactions. They made rules regulating the price of articles and the quality of goods. They punished the workman who charged more or less than "the just price," or who put out poor articles, or gave short weight.

Everything made was carefully inspected. Certain men, called searchers, were appointed by each guild to see that the

A dishonest London baker being drawn through the streets with a short-weight loaf of bread tied around his neck. (From a thirteenth-century manuscript in the London Guildhall.)

products of the members of the guild came up to the standard decided upon by the guild. They went about regularly to the various shops. If a dyer's work was found to be faulty he was fined, if the number of threads was deficient in a weaver's cloth his looms were destroyed. If a baker sold loaves of bread underweight, or poor in quality, he might be dragged on a sledge through the streets with the short-weight loaf suspended around his neck, or his oven might be demolished. The following is the account of the trial of one John Penrose taken from the records of a vintners' guild:

John Penrose was prosecuted for that he sold red wine, unsound and unwholesome for man, in deceit of the common people, and to the grievous damage of the commonalty [the guild]. The judgment was that said John Penrose shall drink a draught of the same wine that he sold to the common people and the remainder of such wine shall then be poured on the head of said John, and that he shall forswear the calling of vintner forever, unless he can obtain the favor of our lord, the king, as to the same.

The guild did a great deal for its members. If a guildsman was sick or in trouble his guild helped him. If a member of a guild died poor, leaving a widow and children, the guild cared for the family. It also used its influence to promote good behavior among its members. A member might be expelled from a guild for bad conduct. One of the old rules says: "If anyone be a common brawler, or given to quarrels, or be a vagabond, or be guilty of any crime whereby the brethren may incur scandal, he shall be admonished once, twice, or thrice, and the fourth time he shall be wholly expelled from the brotherhood."

Learning a trade took a long time. If a boy of ten or twelve years of age wanted to enter a particular trade, his parents would make a contract with a master of that craft and the boy would become his apprentice for seven years, learning the "mystery" of the trade, for the ways of a trade

183

were kept secret except to members of the guild. During that time the boy received no wages, but was fed, clothed, and lodged in his master's house. He had to promise not to waste his master's time but to be a good, industrious pupil and to obey his master as his father.

An apprentice's life was no easy one, for he was a domestic servant and helper, as well as a learner of a trade, and his hours of work were very long. The master's wife might call upon him for help in the house, and the other workmen might send him on errands. He was expected to take down the shutters of the shop early in the morning and put them up again the last thing at night. He had to scrub the floor and keep the shop clean and in order. He had to take his share in crying, "What d'ye lack? What d'ye lack?" by which the apprentices called the attention of the passer-by to the goods for sale. At night he often slept in the attic, or even under the counter in the shop.

Every ambitious apprentice looked forward eagerly to the time when he could become a master and start in business for himself. When the apprenticeship of the lad was over, he was examined by members of the guild, and if he had done his work as apprentice satisfactorily he was allowed to become a journeyman. He could then journey about from town to town, working wherever he could find an opening, now for this master, now for that, thus learning new ways of doing things and broadening his knowledge of his craft.

An industrious journeyman worked hard and saved his money, so that he might set up a shop in his own home, with apprentices and journeymen of his own to work for him. But

184

A mason and a carpenter doing their masterpieces before one of the judges of the guild.

no journeyman could become a master until he was able to do the kind of work required by his guild. In order to test him the wardens of the guild would set him some piece of work to do. This was called his masterpiece, and he must carry it out entirely by himself in the presence of judges. If they approved his work and found him satisfactory in knowledge and in character they instructed him about his duties as a master, about keeping faith with his craft and being loyal to his guild. Then the journeyman put his hand on the Bible and made his solemn pledge: "I shall truly do and obey all the good rules contained in the book of ordinances. I shall always be obedient to my warden. I shall well and duly pay all my dues and charges, so help me God and His Saints." After paying his fee, the new member became a full-fledged master of his craft and could establish his own shop.

The guilds had many rules governing the relations of the masters, journeymen, and apprentices. A boy apprenticed to one master could not change to another without the consent of the officers of the guild. If he misbehaved his master had the right to punish him. If a master treated an apprentice unkindly the boy could appeal to the guild. If an apprentice ran away during his apprenticeship, his place was kept open for him for a certain length of time; and if he did not return within that time he was punished. No master could tempt away another master's workmen by offering higher wages. If a master had more work to do than he could really accomplish he could temporarily ask for the assistance of another master's workmen. If any master failed to feed and clothe his apprentices well or to instruct them properly in their craft he was tried and punished by the guild.

All the more important guilds had their own halls, beautiful Gothic buildings, in which the affairs of the guild were carried on and where the guildsmen met together on festive occasions. On days of ceremony the walls were gayly decked

The Hall of the Clothmakers' Guild at Ypres, Belgium, one of the most beautiful guildhalls in Europe.

with tapestry and hung with banners on which the arms of the guild were much in evidence.

Most of the guilds had a distinctive uniform—or livery, as it was called—which all members wore when they met together on ceremonial occasions, such as feasts, weddings, and holidays. This livery was gay in color and varied with the fashion of the time and taste of the guild. Usually it

187

Wheelmakers.

Needle and
Thimblemakers.

Candlemakers.

Masons.

*Banners of the
Guilds.*

188

was of two colors—scarlet and green, scarlet and black, scarlet and deep blue —the right side of one color and the left of the other. When complete the costume consisted of a hood and a gown, but sometimes only the hood was worn. The guilds also had banners on which were emblems showing the tools of their craft and a motto. The motto of the hammermen of one town was:

> *By hammer and hand
> All arts do stand.*

Every guild had its patron saint, and on that saint's day the members of the guild, clad in their picturesque livery and bearing aloft their banner, marched together in procession to the church for the service, and afterward they had a feast in their guildhall.

Hatters.

Glassmakers.

Painters.

Pastrymakers.

*Banners of the
Guilds.*

In the Days of the Guilds

The thirteenth, fourteenth, and fifteenth centuries were the golden age of the guilds, but later they lost their influence. As long as work was carried on in each little town independently of the rest of the country, the guilds were important. But expanding trade and industry grew too broad for the guilds in the towns to manage. So gradually the guilds lost their usefulness and were given up. But while they lasted the craftsmen of the Middle Ages produced beautiful work, much of which still remains in Europe today for people to enjoy.

XVIII

The Guildsmen Give Their Plays

THE guilds gave plays called mystery, or miracle, plays. You remember that early in the Middle Ages the church began giving little plays of Bible scenes on certain festive days. From this religious ceremony the people got the idea of representing stories from the Bible in the form of plays. When the churchyards could no longer accommodate the spectators the plays were given up by the church and taken over by the guilds.

The summer festival of Corpus Christi, a day of magnificent church parades, was the favorite day for the guilds to give their plays. They were acted on portable stages mounted on wheels, which were dragged from one place to another in the town, so that the play might be given in different places and as many people as possible might see it. These stages were called pageants. They consisted of two stories. The lower story was enclosed by curtains and was used as a dressing room by the actors. The upper story was the stage upon which the acting took place. There was a trapdoor between them through which the actors climbed and arranged themselves, as the wagon made its way about the town.

190

A craft guild giving their play at Coventry, England. The rude platform on wheels on which the plays were given was drawn about from one part of the town to another so that as many people as possible might see them.

In any play in which evil spirits had some dismal task to perform they made their entrance through an opening known as Hell Mouth, a hideous, gaping dragon's head

191

made of linen painted red, with glaring eyes and movable jaws worked by two men, lined with rows of long projecting teeth. It was lighted to look as if it were full of fire, and from it issued smoke and flames. In the course of the play

Hell Mouth.

the red-covered devil and his imps, with the ugliest heads possible, with great horns and hoofs and long tails, leaped out from Hell Mouth to seize wicked characters and drag the unfortunate victims within the cavernous mouth to the

192

infernal regions. Then would issue forth groans and horrible outcries and the clanking of chains, as smoke and flame poured out from the hideous red jaws. Sometimes a devil jumped off the stage and ran among the audience, spreading terror among the good folk as he played pranks upon them.

The guilds took great pride in giving their plays. They presented the chief scenes from the Scriptures, beginning with the creation. Each guild presented a single scene from the Bible story, choosing the one that was best suited to its craft. The shipwrights presented the building of the ark; the mariners, the flood; the goldsmiths, the story of the three kings; and so on.

Early in the morning when the plays were to be given, the narrow streets of the little town were filled with eager spectators, gathered in different places. There were some folk of high rank among the crowd, but for the most part they were made up of the tradesmen and artisans. The guild members have assembled at the appointed place and are dressing for their parts. A herald, richly dressed in livery and holding aloft a banner, is coming down the street. This is the signal that the first pageant is coming. Soon it rolls into sight, drawn by men or horses, pausing at some spot long enough to give its play and then passing on to another neighborhood, where the performance is repeated. Meanwhile a second wagon has rolled up, taking the place left by the first wagon. By this arrangement, in the course of the long summer's day the spectators in each place could see all the plays in their right order. First came the creation, followed by the flood, scenes from the lives of Abraham and

193

Isaac, and on through the Old Testament. The New Testament was represented by scenes from the life of Christ. Thus play followed play until twilight, when a herald announced, "More may not be played for lack of day."

Of all the plays given by the guildsmen none made such an appeal as the nativity plays given by the shepherds, commemorating the birth of Christ. In these simple little plays three shepherds were represented as watching their flocks by night and talking together about the hard times, the heavy taxes, the cold weather, and so on. They lie down to rest, and suddenly a bright star shines out in the heavens. They are startled. One of them says:

> *Brothers, look up and behold!*
> *What thing is yonder that shineth so bright?*
> *As long as ever I watched my fold*
> *Yet saw I never such a sight.*

Then the angel Gabriel appears to them, singing Gloria in Excelsis, and speaks to them:

> *Rise, herdsmen, gentle, attend ye,*
> *For now is He born.*
> *God is made your friend*
> *Now on this morn.*
> *Thus he doth command—*
> *To Bethlehem go, see*
> *Where lieth Thy Lord*
> *In a manger so lowly*
> *Where twain beasties stand.*

194

Guided by the star the shepherds make their way to Bethlehem. There, in a lowly stable, they find the Christ child with Mary, his mother. Filled with tenderness and awe, they fall upon their knees before the child and worship him, and they give him their simple gifts—the only things they have. The first has only his shepherd's pipe to give. He offers it, saying to Mary:

> *I have nothing to give thy child*
> *But my pipe*
> *Wherein much pleasure have I found.*

Then, turning to the child, he says:

> *And now to honor Thy glorious birth*
> *Thou shalt have it to make Thee mirth*
> *Hold! Take it in Thy hand!*

The second shepherd gives a spoon, saying:

> *Hail, Thee, maker of the star,*
> *That went before us!*
> *Hail, Thee, blessedful Bairn,*
> *Lo, Son, I bring thee a flagot.*
> *There hangs there a spoon*
> *To eat thy pottage withal at noon,*
> *As I myself full oft times have done.*

And the third poor shepherd says:

> *Hail, sovereign Savior, for Thou have we*
> *   sought;*
> *Hail, Child and Flower, that all things*
> *   hath wrought;*
> *Thee, have I no things to give*
> *That are worth anything at all*
> *Save my good heart, while I live,*
> *And my prayers till death me doth call.*

Mary thanks all three shepherds gently and says that she
will pray her child to bless them. One of the shepherds says:

> *Brethren, let us all three*
> *Singing, walk homewards.*
> *Unkind will I never more be*
> *But preach ever that I can*
> *As Gabriel by his grace taught me.*

And so that play of the shepherds ends, as they return
home rejoicing.

In a number of plays there was a good deal of funmaking.
The characters and the plots still remained biblical, but new
elements were added so that they became a queer patchwork
of fact and fancy. Humorous scenes were hailed everywhere with delight, the simple people of the day seeing
nothing irreverent in this mingling of religion and amusement. In one version the shepherds were tending their
flocks; they were joined by a neighbor, Mak by name,

whose reputation for honesty was none too good. The shepherds are weary and go to sleep. When the others are snoring Mak rises, seizes a fat sheep, and carries it home to his wife Gill. His wife is alarmed, for in that day sheep stealing was punishable by death, and she is afraid that the other shepherds will suspect Mak when they find that a sheep is missing. She finally decides that the best plan is to wrap the sheep in swaddling clothes like a new-born babe and hide it in the cradle.

Mak hurries back to the shepherds and finds them still sleeping. When they wake he pretends to be sleeping so soundly that they have difficulty in rousing him. Mak then goes home and soon afterward the shepherds discover that a sheep is missing. Suspecting Mak, they follow him home and find him sitting near the cradle of his new-born babe singing a lullaby. They charge him with having stolen the sheep, but he indignantly denies the accusation. The shepherds search the house for the missing sheep, but, finding no trace of it, are about to leave, when one of them, feeling rather ashamed of their suspicion, turns back and asks leave to kiss the new baby. Mak endeavors to keep him away from the cradle, saying:

> *Nay, go way; he slepys,*
> *When he wakyns he wepys.*
> *I pray you go hence.*

But, in spite of this, the shepherd lifts the coverlet, and as he bends over the cradle, he sees the sheep and says, "It is a long-nosed baby." Then Mak and his wife protest that the child has been changed into a sheep by an elf. The shepherds, however, decide to punish Mak. They seize him and toss him in a blanket till they are exhausted and Mak is dizzy. Then, taking the sheep, they return to their hillside and, as dusk gathers, they fall asleep again until they are roused by the sound of the angel announcing the birth of Christ.

In the play about the flood, Noah's wife refuses to go into the ark, and a quarrel follows between her and Noah. At first Noah tries persuasion, saying, "Good wife, doe now as I thee bydd." But the wife is obstinate. She doesn't think it is going to rain and she doesn't want to leave her gossips. Noah warns her of the thunder and lightning: "Therefore, wife, have done. Come into the ship fast." But all arguments are in vain. At last Noah's sons decide to use force to get their mother into the ark.

> *In feith, mother, yet you shall*
> *Whether you will or not*

they say to her, pulling her aboard just in time to avoid the flood.

When his wife is safely on board Noah tries to pacify her. But the enraged wife gives him a resounding blow. This little by-play between Noah, a hen-pecked husband, and his shrewish wife never failed to bring shouts of delighted laughter from the audience.

198

From Medieval to Modern Times

XIX

Caravans and Cargoes

WE HAVE described the life of the people of western Europe in the thousand years that followed the collapse of the Roman Empire. During that time a wonderful new civilization was built up on the ruins of the ancient world. But everything in the world is always changing, and in the fourteenth, fifteenth, and sixteenth centuries people began turning away from the life and ideals that had satisfied them for centuries and looking at the world in a different spirit. New ideas were taking root, new classes of society were becoming more powerful, new knowledge and widened opportunities were making the lives of the people very different from what they had been before. So great was the effect of all these changes that it seemed as if civilization itself was being reborn. Hence the time which witnessed this great awakening in Europe is known as the Renaissance, which means rebirth. But nothing in the world really happens suddenly. Even changes which appear to be sudden have a long story behind them. Let us now trace the history of some of the most important happenings in Europe, which brought to a close the picturesque but narrow medieval world and laid the foundation of our own time.

Up to the eleventh century life in most parts of Europe centered about the castles. The people of each castle, as we have seen, raised their own food, made their own clothes, and provided themselves with most of the things they needed. Except for the yearly fairs in the near-by towns and the occasional visits of traveling merchants there was little trade with the outside world.

There were wonderful civilizations in Asia, but the people of Europe, shut off from them by barriers of high mountains, barren plains, and burning deserts, for many centuries knew little about them. But from quite early times silk and some other things from Asia had found their way to Europe. Then, in the eleventh century, came the Crusades, which greatly increased trade with the East. During two hundred years the Crusaders traveled to Palestine and saw in the bazaars there many strange and beautiful things they had never dreamed existed. They saw finely woven fabrics of cotton, silk, velvet, and damask; beautiful rugs; sweet-smelling perfumes; exquisitely carved ivory; precious stones; delicate wines; delicious fruits—dates, figs, peaches, apricots; and fragrant spices—cinnamon, cloves, ginger, nutmeg and pepper—used for seasoning food and for preserving it.

All these useful and beautiful things gave the people of Europe new tastes in food, new fashions in clothes, and new ideas of comfort in their homes. When the Crusaders returned to Europe they wanted to have many of the things they had come to know in the East. Here was an opportunity for trade, and enterprising merchants were soon bringing to Europe many luxuries from the East.

The overland journeys from Asia were made of long

Traders in Asia carrying merchandise on the backs of camels to the coast of the Mediterranean Sea where it was loaded on ships and taken to Europe. (From Thevet, *Cosmographie universelle,* 1575.)

trains of slow-moving camels heavily laden with boxes and bales of merchandise. Many merchants would travel together in long caravans for greater safety, because the

203

routes were infested by robbers. The goods changed hands many times before they reached Europe. The Eastern merchants took them for part of the way, then they were sold to other merchants who carried them farther. Then they were sold again. Sometimes they were a year or two on the way before they reached the shore of the Mediterranean. As each merchant through whose hands the goods passed had to have his profit, these Eastern goods were very costly by the time they reached Europe. On the shore of the Mediterranean Sea the camels were unloaded and their precious burdens put on ships and carried to Venice. From Venice they were taken over the various trade routes to different parts of Europe.

In many lines of achievement China was far ahead of the people in Europe in medieval times. There were beautiful cities in which were the shops and warehouses of merchants who traded with the whole Eastern world, and in the harbors were fleets of junks laden with spices and precious woods, perfumes, and silks. In the thirteenth century China was ruled over by Kublai Khan, one of its greatest rulers, and under him China came to the height of her magnificence.

Among the merchants of Venice were Maffeo and Nicolo Polo. Having heard of the riches of far-off Cathay, as China was called in those days, they decided to journey there. In 1271 they set off from Venice, taking with them Nicolo's young son, Marco, a lad of seventeen.

The Polos crossed the Mediterranean Sea to Constantinople and then traveled by land, sometimes on horses, sometimes on camels, and sometimes afoot. All along the way they marveled at the splendor of the lands through which they passed, which was far beyond anything known

The Polos setting out for Cathay. (From *Livre des Merveilles*, a fifteenth-century book.)

in Europe at that time. For three years they traveled and finally reached the court of Kublai Khan.

For seventeen years the Polos lived at the court of Kublai

Khan. The emperor took a special interest in young Marco and made him an official of his court and commissioned him to go on many journeys to different parts of his empire. Far and wide Marco traveled in the widespread domain of the Khan and even beyond it into strange lands where no European had ever been. Marco noted everything in the little-known countries through which he traveled. Nothing escaped his keen eyes. Thus he accumulated a vast store of information about the civilization of the lands in the East.

At last the Polos felt a longing for their native land. So they bade farewell to the Khan, and after a long and wearisome journey three bronzed and shabby strangers, dressed in strange Tartar garments, arrived in Venice. Greatly changed in looks, and speaking their own language with difficulty after their many years in the East, they had great trouble in making themselves known. Even their friends and relatives did not recognize them. It did not seem possible that these shabby-looking men could be the Polos, whom they had long since thought to be dead.

To dispel all doubts the Polos decided upon a novel scheme. They invited their kinsfolk and friends to a banquet. When the guests arrived, the Polos, instead of being dressed in their travel-stained garments, appeared in magnificent robes of crimson damask reaching to the floor. When the feast was over Marco went into an adjoining room and returned shortly with the garments the Polos had worn when they arrived in Venice. With a sharp knife he began ripping the seams and tearing out the linings, and before the dazzled eyes of the company out tumbled a great quantity of sapphires, diamonds, rubies, emeralds, and other gems of fabulous value that had been concealed in the garments. It was by this means that the Polos had brought them safely on the long dangerous journey from the East. At the sight of so much wealth everyone was convinced that the three strangers really were "these worthy gentlemen of the house of Polo that they claimed to be."

News of Marco's strange adventures in the East spread through Venice. Many people came to visit him and never tired of listening to his recital of the wonders of the East. So often in his tales did Marco use the word million in describing the wealth, or the distance, or the numbers, in the domain of the Khan that he was nicknamed "Messer Marco il Millione," meaning Mr. Marco of the Millions.

At that time Genoa and Venice were rivals for the rich trade that had sprung up with the East, and four years after the return of the Polos to their native city the fleets of the two cities were engaged in a battle and Marco Polo was given command of a Venetian galley. In the battle the Venetians were completely defeated, and Marco Polo and many other Venetians were captured and sent to prison in Genoa. This was a sad thing for him but a fortunate circumstance for the world, for in a dungeon, to break the monotony of his prison days, he dictated the story of his travels in the East to a fellow captive, one Rustiano of Pisa, a man of some learning, who, fortunately, had learned to write.

Day after day the scribe wrote down the long, adventurous story, describing kingdom after kingdom that Marco had seen, and thus preserved it for all time. He opened the book with the following preface:

Great princes, emperors, and kings, dukes, knights and people of all degrees, who desire to get knowledge of the various races of mankind and the diversities of the sundry regions of the world, take this book and cause it to be read to you. For ye shall find therein all kinds of wonderful things according to the descriptions of Messer Polo, a wise and noble citizen of Venice, as he saw them with his own eyes. For let me tell you that never hath there been a man, be he Christian, or pagan, or Tartar, or man of any nation, who in his own person hath had so much knowledge of the world and its wonders as hath this noble and illustrious citizen of Venice, Messer Polo. And for that reason he bethought himself that it would be a very great pity did he not cause to be put in writing all the great marvels that he had seen so that other people who had not these advantages might by his book get such knowledge.

The riches of the East were vividly set forth. Of Ceylon the book says:

You must know that rubies are found in this island and in no other country of the world but this. They find there also sapphires and topazes and amethysts and many other stones of great price. And the king of this island possesses a ruby which is the finest and biggest in the world. I will tell you what it is like. It is about a palm in length and as thick as a man's arm. It is quite free from flaw and as red as fire.

In the strait between Ceylon and India Marco came upon pearl fishers diving and bringing up shells full of beautiful
208

pink pearls. In the Spice Islands he saw "pepper as white as snow as well as black, in great quantities. In fact the riches of those islands is something wonderful, whether in gold or precious stones, or in all manner of spicery." He went to Cipango, as Japan was called. "The quantity of gold they have is endless," he says, "for they find it in their own islands." The emperor "hath a very large palace which is entirely roofed with fine gold. Moreover, all the pavement of the palace and the floors of its chambers are entirely of gold, in plates like slabs of stone a good two fingers thick, and the windows also are of gold, so that altogether the riches of this palace are incalculable."

Thus the Book of Ser Marco Polo brought to the knowledge of the people of Europe riches beyond anything they had dreamed of, and stirred widespread interest in the little-known lands of Asia. For many years after the book was written kings dreaming of empires, mariners dreaming of adventurous voyages, and merchants dreaming of profits all eagerly read the accounts of the magnificence of the East and the splendors of Cathay, as set forth by Marco Polo, and his book had a great influence upon the later history of the world, as we shall see.

XX

Towns Grow Important

As TRADE increased the towns of Europe became more and more important. In the early part of the Middle Ages most towns were under the protection of the nobles, and their government of them was often very despotic. So it usually became necessary, sooner or later, for a town to settle with its arrogant overlord. Hard and prolonged fighting was often the only way of obtaining justice, but if the townsfolk could succeed in shutting the gates of the town against the lord's followers they might hope to get concessions. The feudal owner might refuse them and quite likely would lay siege to the town, but with the protection of their strong walls there was always a chance that before the noble was able to force the townspeople to open their gates they might make some advantageous terms with him.

These terms were easier to win if the people of the town had money to give in exchange for the favors they asked. The noble who owned the town was sure to need money sometime, and the people of the town would agree to give it to him in return for certain rights or privileges. When the townsmen got these rights they had them set forth in a charter. (The word charter comes from the Latin word *carta,* meaning a piece of paper.) The charter of a town was a paper giving a list of the things the inhabitants could do without asking permission from the lord. In this way the towns gradually made themselves free from the nobles.

The siege of a medieval town. A feudal lord and his followers, whose tents may be seen at the left, are attacking a walled town. The drawbridge at the main gate is up and the portcullis down and town officials in the tower above the gate are listening to a summons to surrender. (From a German woodcut of the sixteenth century.)

After the people of a town gained possession of it the influential citizens organized the government of the town. The leading burghers formed a council, presided over by the burgomaster—or mayor—and made laws for the improvement of the town and plans for its defense. Thus each little town was like a little independent self-governing state, with its own life and institutions.

In castle days there was little money in circulation. As the peasants did all the work the lords were supplied with laborers without paying them wages, and the serfs had their homes and their keep in return for their services. Under such circumstances there was little need for money. But with the steady growth of trade and industry the importance of money constantly increased. Merchants often needed large amounts to carry out some enterprise, and if they did not have it they had to borrow it from someone who did.

People who had a surplus of money might be willing to lend it if they received interest for it, but during most of the Middle Ages there was widespread prejudice against lending money for profit. The medieval church condemned it as sinful, and "usury," as the accepting of even a moderate rate of interest was called, was forbidden by the laws of the church. The business of lending money, therefore, fell largely into the hands of the Jews, and they became the moneylenders of the Middle Ages. Much of the trade of that time was built up on money borrowed from Jews. As many of the loans were not paid back they charged high interest on loans. All this led to prejudice against them on the part of Christians. They were compelled to live in a certain quarter of a town, called the Jewry, and were required to wear a cap, or a badge, which made them easily recognized and exposed them to insult.

As time passed the sentiment of the church changed, and

the prejudice against moneylending died down. By the fifteenth century it was no longer thought wrong for Christians to lend money. The goldsmiths became the first Chris-

A merchant working at his accounts. (From a sixteenth-century woodcut.)

tian moneylenders. As there were no banks it became the custom for merchants to leave their surplus money with a friendly goldsmith for safekeeping, as the goldsmiths had

213

strong vaults in which they kept their precious metals and jewels. The goldsmiths found that the money left with them sometimes remained in their hands for a long time. So they began lending out some of it to people who needed money and were able to pay interest. It was in this way that the goldsmiths became the first bankers. The Medici, the famous goldsmiths of Florence, became the most important bankers in Europe during the Renaissance.

The growth of trade brought an increase in the number of craftsmen in the towns. As time passed and wealth increased many imported articles, that had at first been luxuries enjoyed only by the very rich, came to be necessities to well-to-do people, and the demand for them became so great that it was not long before the workers in the towns began imitating them and they found ever-growing markets for the things they made. Thus new industries of many kinds grew and flourished in the towns.

The towns were the centers of new ideas and new enterprises. To them came merchants from other countries, bringing strange tales of distant lands as well as goods to sell. Inns were built, and travelers meeting at them exchanged stories of the experiences and adventures. In the streets and the market places the people heard the news of the day. The merchants of the towns traveled to faraway places and saw other parts of the world and gained new ideas from different countries.

Wealth brought a desire for the refinements of life. Wealthy merchants and bankers built beautiful palaces and lived in princely style. They were, as a rule, liberal with their money. They had a great pride in their towns and used their wealth to build beautiful buildings and churches for them. They encouraged art by giving money to painters and sculptors. They supported poets. They bought the beautiful

A scene at an inn in the late Middle Ages. (From a sixteenth-century woodcut.)

books made by the monks. Some of them became scholars and delighted in study and translation of old manuscripts. They founded schools and libraries, and did many other things for the improvement of their towns.

215

So all over Europe there were growing up free, self-governing towns, rich and beautiful, the centers of industry, trade, and finance. Because it was situated fortunately for trade, midway between the East and the West, Venice early became the most important port for gathering the luxuries of the East and sending them all over Europe. Along her canals rose the splendid marble palaces of her merchants, and the Rialto, the commercial exchange of Venice, became the business center of the world. Genoa, Pisa, Florence, and Milan also became flourishing cities in Italy. In the south of Germany towns like Augsburg and Nuremberg, through which passed highways from Italy, grew rich. There were also trading cities in northern Germany—Lubeck, Hamburg, and Bremen. In England London, which ever since the days of the Romans had been an important town, was becoming a city of busy streets and workshops, and in France Paris was growing as a center of trade. In the Netherlands towns like Bruges, Ghent, Ypres, and Antwerp sent their manufactures all over Europe.

By the fifteenth century the town had taken the place of the castle as the center of European life. In the towns a new principle of work became important. The people of the castles worked to satisfy their own needs. The people of the towns were engaged in supplying the ever-growing market for new things brought about by trade and industry. Wealth, instead of meaning land gained and held by force, as it meant when the feudal barons were in power, was coming

216

to mean the possession of money which came from buying and selling.

As money became more and more important, the people

Fourteenth-century Venice when she was at the height of her greatness as the center of European trade with Asia. (From a manuscript in the Bodleian Library at Oxford, England.)

possessing money became more important. Thus there grew up in the towns a new class of people. Before the growth of towns there had been only three classes of society: the nobles,

217

the churchmen, and the peasants. The townsfolk, engaged in industry and trade, formed a new class, the middle class, which steadily increased in numbers and influence. In this way the feudal aristocracy of earlier days was being gradually changed into a commercial middle-class society. The nobles thought themselves far above the merchants and felt that to engage in any kind of business was unworthy a gentleman. So they continued to dwell arrogantly in their castles, while the merchants of the towns grew rich from their trade.

XXI

From Force to Law

DURING feudal days society was built up on the principle of force. Most of the land was held by a comparatively few men who had absolute power over the masses of the people. But during the centuries of the Middle Ages, especially in England, the people, through slow but determined progress, won constitutional liberty and secured a government based upon law rather than upon force. This was England's greatest contribution to civilization during the Middle Ages.

One important step in government was the improvement in methods of administering justice adopted in the twelfth century by Henry II, the grandson of William the Conqueror. For centuries the people of Europe had had several strange methods of deciding upon the guilt or innocence of people accused of crime. Feudal ideas of justice were influenced by the religious ideas of the time. The widespread belief was that God would not allow an innocent person to be punished, and various methods were used to ascertain the judgment of God. These were all conducted by the church.

One of these was called the ordeal by fire. A piece of iron was heated in the fire by a priest until it was red hot. Then

219

the priest sprinkled holy water on it and recited a prayer: "The blessing of God, the Father, the Son, and the Holy Ghost descend upon this iron for the discovering of the right judgment of God." Then the iron was placed in the right hand of the accused person, and he took three steps carrying it and threw it to the ground. His hand was then bound for three days. If at the end of that time his hand had "a blister half as large as a walnut," it was regarded as proof of guilt; if the wound was healed the accused person was thought to be innocent and was acquitted, for it was believed that God had proved his innocence. Instead of carrying the iron, the accused person was sometimes blindfolded and made to walk barefoot over red-hot plowshares, while the priest offered a prayer.

Sometimes an accused person was bound hand and foot and thrown into a pool of water, and the priest addressed the water: "I adjure thee, O thou water, that thou do not in any manner receive this man if he be guilty of what he is accused of." If the man sank he was considered innocent and was quickly rescued and set free; but if the water refused to receive him and he floated, his guilt was proved. This was called the ordeal by water.

The warlike nobles did not often undergo trial either by fire or by water. They engaged in what was called the ordeal by battle. A knight who believed that he had been wronged by another knight would throw down his gauntlet, which was taken up by the accused. Then a judge would set a time and place for them to fight a combat. God was asked to show which one was right. If the accuser was beaten it was proof that his accusation was false; if he came off victor it was believed that God had intervened in his behalf.

Trial by combat. (From *Cérémonies des Gages de Bataille,* a fifteenth-century manuscript.)

Such methods of trying people seem very strange to us today, for in none of them was there any attempt to find out

221

the facts about a crime. In time doubt as to the wisdom of them spread, as it was discovered that many wrongdoers, whom everybody knew to be guilty, escaped punishment. In 1215 the church was forbidden to conduct trials by ordeal.

Henry II brought into being a new kind of trial in England, which made it easier for people to have justice done them. He believed that the way to get at the truth about a person's guilt or innocence was to examine witnesses who knew the facts. He arranged that royal judges should make regular circuits through the realm, visiting one place after another to hold court. In each district judges were to select "twelve good men and true," usually neighbors of the parties concerned in the dispute, to investigate the facts. They talked with the man himself, they inquired of his neighbors concerning him, and examined any objects that would help them to learn the truth. Then they were sworn to "a true verdict give." To these men was given the name "jurors," from the Latin word, "juro," meaning "I swear." This was the beginning of trial by jury. A little later on witnesses were called to tell the jury facts they might know about the case. Thus the English law courts developed in the twelfth century.

The decisions of these courts year after year and century after century gradually shaped the common law of England, which protected the life, liberty, and property of people. Trial by jury was one of the greatest steps in the liberty of the people, because it gave an accused man the benefit of the unprejudiced opinion of twelve men as to his guilt or innocence, and gave this right to even the humblest and

One of the early law courts in England.

weakest in the realm. It also was a step forward in estab-
lishing law and order by doing away with private warfare,

223

because one of the reasons the nobles fought so much during the Middle Ages was because there was no other way of settling disputes.

Another important step was taken early in the thirteenth century during the reign of King John. John, the brother of Richard the Lionhearted, who had tried to seize the throne while Richard was away on the Crusades, followed Richard as king and proved to be one of the worst rulers England ever had. It happened, however, that by his very wickedness he did a great service to his country and to civilization, by bringing about greater political liberty for the people.

When John became king he levied taxes unjustly, and in other ways oppressed his people. Again and again he demanded large sums of money, and his subjects were afraid to refuse them because they knew that if they did they would be severely punished. Enemies of the king were thrown into prison and kept there indefinitely without being tried to find out whether they were guilty of any offense. Lands and goods were illegally seized. Not even the highest nobles were free from fines and taxes of the most tyrannical kind.

Finally the important barons of the realm decided to endure John's oppressive government no longer. Stephen Langton, Archbishop of Canterbury, became a leader in the revolt against the king. One day he called together several barons who were in the cathedral and, according to Roger of Wendover, a chronicler of the time, said, "There has been found a charter of Henry I by which, if ye will, ye may recall to their former estate, the liberties ye have so long lost," and he read the long-forgotten document to them.

224

Henry I was the son of William the Conqueror. He had drawn up a charter in which he had promised to rule his people justly according to the old Anglo-Saxon customs. When the barons heard the promises made by a king a hundred years before to their ancestors they decided to stand up for their rights. Kneeling before the altar of an old Saxon saint they swore a solemn oath to compel the king, by force of arms if necessary, to restore the liberties of the realm.

John tried in every way to avoid a struggle with the barons, but it was of no use. Finally he sent a messenger to them, asking what liberties they sought. The barons sent back a list of demands. When these were read to John he cried out in wrath, "Why, amongst all these unjust demands, did not the barons ask for my kingdom also? I will never grant liberties that would render me their slave."

The messenger carried the king's refusal back to the waiting barons, but the stern barons, who had suffered so much at John's hands, were firm in their determination to end his tyranny. All the nobles and churchmen united against him. Even his most trusted followers saw that his cause was hopeless and abandoned him. Seeing the uselessness of resistance, the wretched king sent a messenger to the barons, "that for the sake of peace and for the welfare and honour of his realm he would freely concede to the laws and liberties which they asked and that they might appoint a place and a day for him and them to meet for the settlement of these things."

A broad stretch of meadowland, known as Runnymede, on the Thames River, not far from London, was chosen as

225

the meeting place. The insurgent nobles marched from London, their armor glistening in the bright sun, their banners flying, and gathered two thousand strong. The royal tent was pitched near by. In that same meadow the Anglo-Saxons had been wont to gather to discuss questions of unusual importance. And there in that meadow, consecrated to freedom by its ancient associations, on June 15, 1215, John unwillingly affixed his great seal to the charter which the nobles had prepared. It began:

John, by the grace of God, King of England, Lord of Ireland, Duke of Normandy and Aquitaine and Earl of Anjou, to the archbishops, earls, barons, and others, his faithful subjects, greeting.

Know ye that we, in the presence of God and for the health of our soul and the souls of our ancestors and heirs, to the honor of God and the exaltation of the Holy Church and by the advance of our venerable fathers and liegemen, of our own free will and pleasure have granted and confirmed this our present charter which we shall observe and do will it to be faithfully observed by our heirs forever.

We have also granted to all freemen of our kingdom, for us and for our heirs forever, all the underwritten liberties, to have and to hold, they and their heirs forever of us and our heirs.

Thereafter followed sixty-three provisions, many of which, though important in their day, do not apply to later times, but among them were two which came to play an important part in later history. Many people had been thrown into prison and kept there without trial. That was

226

never to happen again, for the charter declared: "No free-man shall be seized or imprisoned or dispossessed, or out-lawed, or in any way brought to ruin, except by the legal judgment of his peers and by the law of the land." It de-clared an accused man entitled to a just and speedy trial: "To no man will we sell or deny right, or delay right or justice." In those passages the king admitted that he had no right to imprison or punish any of his subjects except in accordance with the law.

The people had been unjustly taxed. As a means of pre-venting this in the future it was stated in the charter: "No scutage [tax] or aid shall be raised except by the general council of the kingdom." By this provision in the charter the king was obliged to get the consent of the chief nobles to taxation.

"I am a king with five-and-twenty over-kings," cried John, in a burst of fury, when he read this provision.

Many copies of the charter were made and were sent to every church of the kingdom to be read to the people, and there was great rejoicing throughout the realm.

It is said that when John signed the charter he wore a smiling countenance and declared that he was entirely satisfied with the settlement of affairs, but that when he was safely back in the privacy of his castle he gave vent to rage, gnashing his teeth like a madman, throwing himself on the floor, and gnawing the rushes with which it was strewn. But his rage soon passed. He had signed the charter because he could not help himself, but he had no intention of keep-ing his promises. In a few months he had brought foreign

227

troops to England and put himself at their head, and the barons marched against him with their followers. At first John was successful everywhere. He went through England burning and ravishing the country, but the struggle between the barons and the tyrant king was brought to an end in a few years by John's death.

No doubt the barons had only their own interests in mind in forcing John to sign the Magna Carta, but whatever they may have had in their minds they established the great principle that the king was subject to the law of the land. In the charter it was set down in black and white that the people had certain rights and that a king had certain duties toward his people.

The charter was disregarded not only by John but by other despotic kings later on, but the people always clung to it as the guarantee of their liberty and time and time again forced their tyrannical rulers to observe its articles. "From the time the charter was first shown to the people," says Roger of Wendover, "it carried all men with it. There was but one voice and one mind; all would stand as a wall in defense of the liberties of the realm."

XXII

England, Mother of Parliaments

THE thirteenth century, which opened with the winning of the Great Charter, was also the time when England laid the foundation of representative government.

In the very early days in England the Anglo-Saxons introduced there a custom which was of great importance to later civilization. They lived in small villages and whenever it was necessary to consider important affairs of the community, all the men of the village met together under the branches of some spreading oak tree. Every man in the meeting had a right to say what he thought and to vote as he thought best. Laws were drawn up by a council of the older, wiser men and put before the assembly. A clashing of spears on shields meant that the law was pleasing to the people, a murmur of discontent showed that it was not and caused the law to be cast aside or changed.

This assembly—or town-moot, as it was called—had to do only with the affairs of one village or town. A group of villages large enough to supply a hundred warriors was called a hundred. Once a month there was a hundred-moot, to which each village sent representatives. As the hundred-moot bound together several villages, the folk-moot discussed questions that were important to the whole tribe. When the tribes became united into one kingdom it was customary for the king to call together the chief men of all the tribes. This assembly was called the Witenagemot, or assembly of wise men.

Under the Norman kings the Witenagemot became the Great Council and was called by the kings from time to time, but it changed its nature. It was no longer a meeting of men representing the people, but a court of the king's chief feudal barons. It had only the appearance of power, for although the king was supposed to govern with the advice of the Great Council, he was not obliged to follow its advice. It was in an effort to make the Great Council more effective that the barons had inserted into the Great Charter the clause requiring the king not to levy taxes without its consent.

King John was followed on the throne by his son, who became Henry III. Henry did not keep his promises any better than his father had kept his. He was extravagant and always in need of money, and to get it he repeatedly promised to obey the charter; but over and over again he broke his word and taxed the people without the consent of the Great Council.

In vain the barons struggled with their unruly king, and finally the rising tide of discontent with his misgovernment broke out into a barons' war similar to that in the reign of John. The leader of the revolt was Simon de Montfort. In the war Henry was taken prisoner, and for a short time Simon de Montfort became head of the government.

230

In the year 1265 Simon de Montfort called a new kind of meeting of the Great Council, which was to bring about a great change in the government of England. Up to that time the Great Council, or Parliament, as it had by this time

Earl Simon de Montfort.

come to be called, had been made up only of important barons and churchmen. Simon de Montfort saw that in order to rule successfully he must rally to his support all classes of people. He therefore thought it advisable to per-

231

mit not only the greatest nobles and churchmen to be present but two knights from every county and two citizens from each of the more important towns. This was the first time in the history of the country that plain citizens had a place in the Great Council, and Simon de Montfort is therefore sometimes called the "Father of the House of Commons."

King Henry was followed on the throne by his son, Edward I, who was a strong king and a good one. He had the wisdom to adopt Simon de Montfort's idea of admitting not only nobles but representatives of the counties and the towns to Parliament. In 1295 he called a meeting of Parliament in which all classes of people were represented. "It is right," he said, "that matters that concern all should be settled by those who can speak for all." Thus Edward established the fundamental principle of representative government, that all who obey the laws should have a voice in the making of the laws.

The Parliament of 1295 is known as the Model Parliament, because it served in most respects as a model for later meetings. In this Parliament it was decided that no general tax could be levied on the nation without the consent of its representatives. The importance of this is very great, because it made the king directly dependent for his revenues upon the good will of the people.

At first the representatives of the counties and towns met with the nobles. Coming as they did from the common people, these representatives were quite weak, as they were greatly overawed by the nobles. The advice of the commons was not asked about anything. They were needed only to

A meeting of the English Parliament in the thirteenth century.

give their consent to taxes. The king's needs were stated to them, and they met by themselves to consider them. Then they returned to Parliament and only one man was allowed to speak for them.

In 1340 came an important step in the development of Parliament when it was divided into two houses: the House of Lords, representing the nobles and higher clergy; and the House of Commons, representing the people of the counties and towns. As time passed and the power of the nobles grew less the House of Lords steadily declined in power, while the House of Commons, representing the rising middle class, became steadily more important and in later centuries became the real power in government.

In the early years Parliament did not meet regularly. It did not make the laws. Its chief business was to settle upon taxes, and the king called it into being only when he needed money. But as time went on Parliament's control of taxation led to greater and greater power. Gradually the members learned to grant the king money only when he was willing to redress the grievances of the people which they pointed out to him. Thus Parliament came to have more and more influence upon the king's policy and was able to secure laws promoting the welfare of the people.

During the Middle Ages the people of England traveled far along the road of political liberty. Their freedom was greater than that enjoyed by any other people of the time. The principles of representative government had taken root there, and the foundations of democracy were laid.

XXIII

The Serfs Become Freemen

THE liberties we have been telling about were for freemen only. They were not for the peasants, and as the peasants made up the mass of the people, most of the people of England still had no voice in their government. But in the fourteenth century the constantly growing feeling for liberty reached even the lowly peasants. They were no longer willing to be obedient, toiling serfs as they had been in earlier days. They wanted better conditions and a greater share in the good things of life, and they began demanding rights and privileges they had never dreamed of before.

Strange to say, this new spirit was strengthened by a dreadful calamity. In the year 1348 a terrible plague, known as the Black Death, swept over Europe, causing the death of thousands and thousands of people. The poor peasants suffered most because they lived in such unsanitary conditions and had the least care. In many places whole villages of peasants were wiped out.

When the scourge was over about half the workers on the estates of the nobles in England had disappeared. With just as many fields to be cared for and half as many peasants there was a great scarcity of labor, and many of the lords no longer had serfs enough to do their work. Their crops were neglected, the herds and flocks strayed over the fields with no one to look after them, and the nobles saw their lands going to ruin. They made desperate efforts to get workers, and many of them offered the peasants wages for their work instead of asking of them the customary feudal services. The peasants, seeing that their labor was now of more value, demanded higher wages; and if these were refused, they frequently deserted their lords and hired themselves out to others who offered them more money.

Then the lords began making laws fixing the rate of wages and ordering punishment for those who demanded more. These laws stirred up bitter discontent among the peasants and were the beginning of a long struggle ending in revolts of the peasants, in which the poor were arrayed against the rich.

A leader of one of these revolts was John Ball, a poor priest, who went about the country preaching that all men were equal and that every man had rights, no matter how humble he might be. John Froissart, the famous chronicler of the Middle Ages, who spent years traveling from place to place gathering his material at first hand, tells the story thus:

In the year of our Lord 1381 there fell in England great mischief and rebellion of the common people. These unhappy people began to stir because they said they were kept in great bondage the which they would no longer suffer, for if they labored or did anything for their lords, they would have wages therefore as well as other men. And in this imagination was a foolish priest in the County of Kent, called John Ball, for this priest used oftentimes on Sundays, after mass, when the people were going out of the ministry, to go into the cloister and preach, and made the people assemble about him, and would say thus:

"Ah, ye good people, matters goeth not well in England, nor shall not do, till everything be common, till there be no villeins nor gentlemen, but we be all united together, and the lords be no greater masters than we be. What have we deserved or why should we be kept thus in bondage? We be all come from one father and mother, Adam and Eve. Whereby can they say or show that they are greater lords than we be, saving by that they cause us to win and labor for that on which they depend?

"They are clothed in velvet and fur, and we be vestured in poor cloth; they have their wines and spices and good bread, and we have the rye, the bran and the drawing out of the chaff and drink water; they dwell in fair houses, and we have the pain and travail, rain and wind in the fields; and by that that cometh from our labors they keep and maintain their estates. We be called their bondsmen, and without we do readily their service, we be beaten.

"Let us go to the king, he is young, and show him what servage we be in, and when the king seeth us we shall have some remedy."

Thus John Ball said on Sundays when the people issued out of the churches in the villages; wherefore many people loved him and they would murmur together, affirming how John Ball said truth.

The archbishop of Canterbury, who was informed of the sayings of John Ball, caused him to be taken to prison to chastise him. And when John Ball was out of prison he returned again to his error as he did before.

So these unhappy people rose and came toward London

to the number of sixty thousand. They had a captain called Wat Tyler, and with him was Jack Straw and John Ball.

The king was counselled that he should issue out to speak to them and the king sent word to them that they should all draw to a fair plain called Mile-end where the people did sport themselves in the summer season, and there he would grant them what they wished.

When the king came to Mile-end he found three score thousand men of divers villages. So the king entered in among them and said to them sweetly, "Ah ye good people, I am your king; what lack ye? What shall ye say?"

Then such as heard him said, "We will that ye make us free forever, ourselves, our heirs, and our lands so that we be called no more bond."

"Sirs," said the king, "I am willingly agreed thereto; withdraw unto your own homes and into such villages as ye came from and I will cause writings to be made and seal them with my seal containing everything that ye demand."

These words appeased well the common people, such as were simple and good plain men, and they said, "It was well said; we desire no better."

Trusting in the king's promise, the peasants went back to their homes, but as soon as Richard had gathered an army he hanged John Ball and the other leaders of the peasants and put down the revolt. When Richard was reproached by the peasants for his faithlessness he replied: "Villeins you were and villeins you are. In bondage you shall abide and that not your old bondage but a worse."

The revolt of the French peasants was worse than the uprising in England. Hard as was the lot of the English serfs, they were much better off than the French peasants, who

238

for many years suffered terribly from feudal oppression. Increased taxation drove them to despair, and the revolt once started spread all over France. In an outburst of blind passion the peasants raged over the land, burning castles and

King Richard addressing the peasants during the peasants' revolt. (From the *Chronicles* of Froissart.)

killing their feudal lords. The nobles avenged themselves by slaughtering the peasants in great numbers.

All the revolts of the peasants were suppressed with great cruelty, and their attempts to gain their freedom seemed to

239

end only in miserable failure. The growth of towns and developing trade, however, broke for many serfs the bonds that bound them to the land. The workers in the towns were much better off than the peasants on the manors. They had better food, better clothes, more comfortable homes. In the towns there was a real chance for a poor man if he worked hard and saved his money. Through his efforts he might rise to almost any place; but for the peasants on the manors there was little chance for advancement; once a peasant always a peasant. The children of peasants became peasants when they grew up. The freedom of the towns therefore attracted many peasants.

The peasants, you remember, were forbidden by law to leave a manor without their lord's permission, but sometimes they tried to gain their freedom by running away. If a peasant ran away his lord could go after him, and if he was caught he was liable to be severely punished. If, however, a peasant succeeded in reaching a town and hiding there undiscovered for a year and a day, he might claim his freedom. "If any serf shall dwell unclaimed for a year and a day in a chartered town so that he hath been received into the community or guild of that town as a citizen," said one of the old laws, "that fact shall free him from villeinage." Many peasants succeeded in doing this and became free working men in the towns.

The increase in the use of money also helped many peasants who remained on the manors to gain their freedom. When money came into circulation the custom of paying wages for services spread. The nobles found that it was much more satisfactory to hire men to work for them than to depend upon serfs who shirked their work whenever possible. The peasants began selling the produce of their farms and paying their lords rent for their houses and fields instead of giving their labor. This change made the serfs much freer than they had ever been before. It gave them liberty to work when and how they chose, and they were not bound to the land as they had been.

Thus, in one way or another, the peasants gradually found their way out of a life of bondage and became free men. By 1450 serfdom had passed away in England and, by the close of the Middle Ages, in most of Western Europe.

XXIV

The Struggle for Religious Liberty

FOR centuries the people of Europe had accepted without question what the church taught them, but the new spirit which was stirring men to think for themselves made itself felt in religion as well as in other phases of life. In the sixteenth century there came a great religious change in Europe, which is called the Reformation, because it was the reforming of the church.

The church had become enormously wealthy and powerful, and there came to be great difference between the ideals of the church and some of its practices. Some of the clergy were worldly. They dressed richly and lived in luxury. Unworthy priests neglected their parishes. Gradually there arose a feeling that the church was using its power for its own advantage instead of for the good of the people. Such ideas destroyed confidence of many people in the church's goodness and wisdom and their reverence for its authority.

Germany took the lead in bringing about the reformation of the church. The chief leader in the movement was a monk, named Martin Luther. Luther was a professor of theology in the University of Wittenberg, where his lectures attracted large audiences.

242

One of the customs of the church which Luther did not approve of was the granting of what were called indulgences. An indulgence was the forgiveness for wrongdoing granted by the church if the sinner would do some good deed or give a gift of money to the church to be used for some holy purpose. Luther objected to this practice, because he saw it led people to believe that they could be forgiven their sins without true repentance. He believed that a sinner could be saved only by a change of heart.

The thirty-first of October, 1517, was the Feast of All Saints, a great day in Wittenberg. An indulgence had been granted to all who visited the church and confessed their sins. On the evening of that day Luther went to the church and posted on the door, so that everyone could see them, ninety-five statements against the practice, asserting that only true penitence could bring forgiveness of sins.

This was the beginning of a long struggle between Luther and the church. At first Luther was still faithful to the church, but as time went on he realized that he differed with it in many other matters. In 1519 he denied the authority of the Pope and appealed to the Bible as the sole authority for belief and conduct.

At first the Pope had paid but little attention to Luther, but as the controversy grew he issued a bull—so called from the lead seal (Latin *bulla*) attached to papal documents—saying that Luther must retract all that he had said or he would be excommunicated. Instead of obeying Luther placed a placard on the walls of the church inviting the students and townspeople to repair at the hour of nine at night to the market place of the town. There a bonfire was made and, as the flames rose, Luther approached and cast into them the Pope's bull. Great was the excitement in the town, and the news spread all over Germany and beyond.

Luther addressing the Diet at Worms. (From an old print.)

Luther was then forced to face trial for heresy in the city of Worms. He bravely faced the princes, nobles, and great dignitaries of the church who had met to pass judgment on him. When he was told that he must give up the opinions the church condemned, he replied in a voice clearly heard by all: "Unless convinced to the contrary by Scripture or

244

by clear reasoning I cannot nor will not revoke anything that I have said, for it is neither safe nor right to act against conscience." The trial proceeded, and for two hours Luther defended himself. Again he was asked to recant, but he replied: "Here I stand; I cannot do otherwise. God help me. Amen."

Thus Luther enunciated a new principle of religion—that a person should believe not what authority told him to believe but what his own conscience told him was right.

As a result of this trial Luther was declared an outlaw. The emperor might put him in prison or sentence him to death. Before coming to Worms, however, Luther had been promised that he might go there and leave in safety, and he made haste to leave the city. On his way back to Wittenberg he was suddenly surrounded by a group of knights, who took him prisoner and carried him off to a lonely castle. These were really his friends in disguise, who took this method of hiding Luther. Luther remained in his castle refuge for a year. During that time he translated the Bible into German, so that everyone could read it. His Bible was printed and soon became famous throughout the country.

Gradually the movement for religious freedom spread to other countries, and most of the people in northern Europe founded new churches of their own. Most of the people of southern Europe, however, remained faithful to the Catholic Church and are so today. The new churches were called Protestant, because they arose as protests against the church which everyone had followed for many centuries.

Long before Luther began his quarrel with the Pope there

had been men in Europe who had protested against the abuses of the church. Among these was John Wycliffe, a teacher at Oxford in the fourteenth century. He began to criticize the church and insisted that men should know the will of God by reading the Bible for themselves. He translated the Bible into English and organized a band of "poor priests" to spread simple truths about the Bible through all England. They went out to every village and hamlet of England to preach to the common people.

The followers of Wycliffe were put down, but his teachings spread beyond England. John Huss, a professor in the University at Prague, in Bohemia, took them up. He was brought before a church council and ordered to recant, but he replied that he could not unless he was convinced that he was in error. He was declared guilty of teaching "many things evil, scandalous, seditious, and dangerously heretical" and was burned at the stake.

When people began studying the Bible and thinking about religion for themselves, differences of opinion arose among the reformers, and the Protestants, therefore, split up into different sects—or denominations. In Germany were the Lutherans, as the followers of Luther were called. In Switzerland the chief leader of the reformers was John Calvin, who was the founder of the Presbyterian Church. Some people came to believe that everyone should be baptized in a certain way, and these people were called Baptists.

To the Catholic Church all these new creeds seemed like terrible heresies, and the church sought to stamp them out
246

through the Inquisition. This was a court presided over by dignitaries of the church, whose duty it was to try people accused of being heretics and to punish them if they were found guilty.

Many good men within the Catholic Church saw the need of correcting things that were wrong with the church but were opposed to lessening the authority of the Pope. The most famous reformer within the church was Ignatius Loyola, a young Spanish nobleman. Loyola devoted his life to the service of the church, and in 1534 formed a religious society called the Society of Jesus, whose members were known as Jesuits. The Jesuits did much missionary work and won back to the Catholic Church many people who had deserted it. Probably from your study of American history you remember the good work of the Jesuit priests in the early days of the New World.

The Reformation was not entirely a religious matter. In several countries it became a struggle between the church and the king as the head of religion. In England King Henry VIII separated from the Catholic Church because the Pope would not grant him a divorce from his queen. In his youth he had been compelled to marry a Spanish princess, Catherine of Aragon, the daughter of Ferdinand and Isabella. Henry had grown tired of Catherine and wanted to marry Anne Boleyn, a maid in waiting at the court. At first he tried to get the Pope to allow him to divorce Catherine. When the Pope refused, he decided to abolish the authority of the Pope in England and make himself head of the church. In 1534 Parliament passed the Act of

247

Supremacy, which declared the English king to be "the only supreme head on earth of the Church of England."

Henry made few changes in the Catholic religion, but after his death a certain form of the Protestant faith called the Church of England was established by law, a uniform service was prepared, and all people were required to attend the new church. Thus England became a Protestant nation.

The Reformation was the cause of cruel persecution, and terrible crimes were committed in the name of religion. People were imprisoned, tortured, and burned at the stake because of their religious beliefs. Catholics persecuted Protestants; Protestants treated Catholics just as harshly, and often they punished other Protestants if they happened to follow a different leader. It was a time of great intolerance. Even governments thought it their right to tell their people what to believe. If a ruler was a Catholic all his subjects had to be Catholics; if he took up one of the new religions his subjects were forced to adopt them also, and those who did not obey were severely punished.

For more than a century the bitter struggle went on. Slowly, however, out of these conflicts grew the realization that each person must decide for himself what faith he will follow and that it is useless to try to force him to accept a form of religion against his will. Some of the old bitterness and intolerance still remain in the world today, but in most civilized countries people of different faiths live peaceably side by side, respecting one another's honest beliefs.

XXV

The First Printed Books

THE books, so slowly and laboriously made by the monks, were very rare and precious. Even wealthy people seldom owned more than one or two of them. Not until a quicker way of making books could be discovered could they be produced in such numbers that everybody could have them.

A new way of making books was introduced into Europe from China, which was a great deal quicker than that of the scribes. For each page of a book the printer cut a block of wood the size of the page he wished and drew upon it whatever picture and words he wanted to print. Then he skillfully cut away the wood, leaving the raised outline of the pictures and letters. The carved block was inked and parchment laid on it and pressed down upon it.

The pages, thus printed, were bound together into a book. Books of this kind were called block books. They were, of course, much cheaper than those made by the monks. The poor people could not afford the beautiful handmade books of the scribes, but these cheap, simple, picture books became very popular.

One of the best known of the block books was the *Biblia Pauperum*—or *Bible of the Poor*. It was a series of forty

A page from the *Biblia Pauperum,* a block book.

pictures representing scenes in the Old Testament and in the
life of Christ, with a few words underneath the pictures

250

explaining them. Another very popular block book was called the *Ars Moriendi,* which means the *Art of Dying.* This was a manual of instructions to people showing sick people how to prepare for death. All through his life a man was supposed to be beset with horrible demons up to his very last breath. The *Ars Moriendi* showed the temptations to which a man would be subjected on his deathbed and how by the aid of divine help he might resist them.

Even with block printing, the making of books was still a slow process, for a block had to be carved separately for each page, and this was such a task that books with only a few pages could be made in this way. Then about the middle of the fifteenth century a new way of printing books was thought out by John Gutenberg, of Mainz, Germany.

Gutenberg had made several block books and found the work very slow. He wondered whether he could not find a quicker way of printing. One day the idea came to him that if each letter of the alphabet was carved separately the letters could be combined to form the words of a book, then the type could be put away ready for use another time. The idea took possession of Gutenberg, and he eagerly went to work, giving all his time and strength and money to trying to find a way of doing this.

Gutenberg tried making the letters of wood, but he found that wood was so soft that it wore out quickly. Then he tried making the letters of metal. First he tried lead, but he found it too soft. Then he tried iron, but that would not work. Then he decided that he must make a combination of metals. After much experimenting he succeeded in doing this. He made a little mold for each letter and then poured the melted metal into it.

When Gutenberg came to print with his metal type he found that pressure was needed to make the impression of the letters. So he invented a printing press similar to the presses that were used for making wine in those days.

Gutenberg's little printing press was a very simple affair. It was just an upright frame to which was attached a big screw which worked up and down. On the lower end of the screw a board was fastened. By turning the screw this board could be forced up and down. The type was set in a wooden frame beneath the board and inked. The paper was laid over the type and the screw turned until the board was forced tightly down on the paper. Then the screw was worked up, the board was lifted with it, and the paper was ready to be taken out with the printing on it.

Gutenberg also had trouble with his ink. The only ink known at the time was that used by the monks. Gutenberg found that when this ink was used in printing it collected in drops and made ugly spots on the paper. Another kind of ink would have to be made for printing. The Italian painters had invented a new paint by mixing lampblack and linseed oil. From them Gutenberg got the idea of a new kind of ink, and it proved satisfactory.

For years Gutenberg worked on his invention, and into it went all the money he had saved. Then came the time when he did not have any more money to carry on his work. A rich goldsmith named Faust—or Fust—helped Gutenberg by lending him money and forming a partnership with

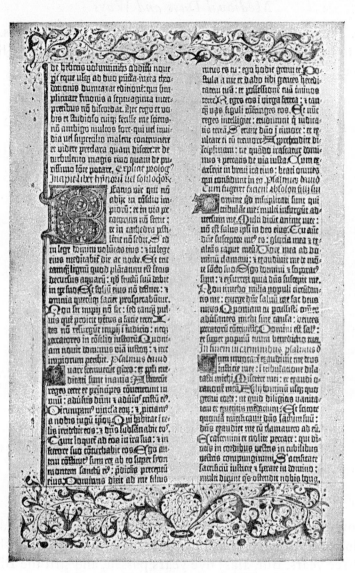

A page from Gutenberg's Bible.

him. Their plan was to print a Bible with the new press. It was to be printed in Latin and was to look in every way like the best of the manuscript books.

A papermaker and his apprentice. (From a sixteenth-century woodcut.)

Joyfully Gutenberg began work. It was a great undertaking. He thought that he would have his Bible finished in three years. But, alas! five years passed, and still the Bible

254

was not finished. Fust had invested a large amount in the enterprise, and no money had come back to him. So he brought suit against Gutenberg to recover the money he had

Early bookmakers at work. (From a sixteenth-century woodcut.)

lent him. The judge decided in Fust's favor. Gutenberg had no money with which to pay the debt, and everything that he possessed—his printing press, his type, the pages of the

Bible that had been printed—all went to Fust. This was a crushing blow to Gutenberg, but he did not give up. He succeeded in securing other help and started work once more. At last, in 1456, after years of hard work, trials, and disappointments, the first printed Bible was finished.

Gutenberg's invention would have been of little value, however, if there had not come to be known in Europe some good cheap material for printing on. Parchment and vellum were expensive and too thick and clumsy for the printing press. Fortunately paper, which was introduced into Europe shortly before the invention of the printing press, proved to be the needed material. Centuries earlier the ingenious Chinese discovered that paper could be made from rags, but they kept the method of making it a secret. But toward the end of the seventh century, as the result of a raid by the Arabs, some Chinese paper makers were taken as prisoners, and from them the Arabs learned how to make paper. In the eleventh century the Moors introduced paper making into Spain, and from there it spread to other countries of Europe. Not until the fourteenth century, however, was paper abundant enough for books to be made cheaply.

After the invention of printing the craft of paper making developed rapidly and mills were set up all over Europe. To make it, large water wheels set in motion a wooden cylinder spiked with heavy wooden projections. As the wheel revolved these projections tilted high up in the air and then dropped with great force and beat torn and well-soaked rags lying in a tub. This was kept up until the rags were beaten to a mass of pulp.

A workman, called a vat man, stood on a platform in front of a vat of pulp, holding a sieve made of fine wire in a rectangular wooden frame. He dipped the frame into the big vat of pulp. When he brought it to the surface it was covered with the pulp which was to form the sheet of paper. As he

An early print shop. (From a woodcut by Stradanus.)

shook it gently to and fro, the water was drained out through the sieve and the fibers of the pulp became matted together.

The next workman, called a coucher, placed the frame upon an incline to allow the excess water to drain off, and when the pulp was the proper consistency the mold was turned over and the moist sheet of paper was deposited upon

257

a piece of wool cloth, or felting. Another felt was placed on top of the sheet, and then another sheet of paper, and so until a hundred or more sheets were formed, each sheet interleaved by a piece of felt. The pile was then placed in a screw press and pressed down to expel as much water as possible. The felts were removed and the paper pressed again. Then the leaves were arranged in a different order and pressed again.

The third workman was the layman, and it was his duty to separate the sheets of felt and place the sheets of paper in a pile. The felt was returned to the coucher to be used again.

The next step was drying. At the top of the old paper mills was the drying loft. The paper was dried by hanging four or five sheets together over ropes stretched across the drying loft, where a current of air could reach them from every side.

The new way of printing, begun in Germany, soon spread to other countries, and before the close of the fifteenth century presses were busy in every country of Europe and books were being produced at a rate undreamed of by the patient monks in the monasteries.

XXVI

Education Spreads among the People

IT WAS a long time after the fall of Rome before the people of Europe had schools and colleges. For several hundred years the only schools were those in the monasteries or connected with the cathedrals, and there was practically no schooling for the mass of the people. But the towns became the centers of education, and in the large towns universities grew up.

The universities of those days had no large buildings as our universities have today. They grew in a very simple way wherever students gathered together to learn from some famous teacher. It was the practice of learned men to go about from town to town teaching. These wandering scholars attracted youths from near and far. In time teachers of different subjects began gathering at important centers. This was a great saving of time for students, because then all subjects could be studied at one place. Each teacher would rent a room and lecture there. Thus a university gradually grew up around great teachers. There were no books for the students. The teacher slowly dictated his lectures, and the students laboriously wrote them down word for word and committed them to memory. There was little or no discussion or criticism.

Some of the universities still in existence today began in this way. One of the first grew up in Paris, where a brilliant young teacher, named Peter Abelard, lived. Thousands of young students, hungry for knowledge, flocked from all parts of Europe to hear him lecture. The fame of Abelard led to an increase of masters and students at Paris and led the way for the establishment of a university there.

Before the end of the twelfth century teachers had become so numerous in Paris that they formed a guild for the advancement of their interests. This was called a universitas—or union—and from it comes our word university. Like a guild a university consisted of the masters, who were the professors, and the students, who corresponded to apprentices and journeymen. After several years of study a student became a "bachelor of arts," which gave him the right to teach certain elementary subjects to younger students. On completing the full course—usually six years in length—the bachelor took his final examinations and presented his thesis, which was his masterpiece. If these were satisfactory he received the degree of "master of arts" and became a master. These degrees are still given by our colleges and universities, although they have long since lost their early significance.

Sometimes groups of students would become discontented and leave one town and go to another. There they would start a new university. Thus the University of Oxford was founded in 1380 by English students and masters from

New College, Oxford, in 1453.

Paris. The University of Cambridge was founded by students and masters from Oxford.

Scholars and learned professors often busied themselves carrying on discussions which seem to us today rather ridiculous. They were trying to answer questions concerning the nature of God and the soul which occupied the minds of most of the people of the time. They often debated such questions as: Can two angels occupy the same place at the same time? Do angels in moving from place to place pass through space?

In the fifteenth century a new field of study was introduced into the universities. In the centuries following the fall of Rome, when the barbarous tribes were overrunning Europe, much of the knowledge and culture of the Greeks and Romans were forgotten; but in Constantinople the ancient learning still lived on and it became the greatest center of learning in Europe. The city was full of scholars who loved and studied the ancient masterpieces of literature, and its library was filled with priceless manuscripts.

In the year 1453 Constantinople fell into the hands of the Turks. At that time many scholars fled, carrying with them precious manuscripts that had been treasured in the library at Constantinople. Many of these fugitive scholars took refuge in Italy and aroused in Italian scholars a new interest in the works of the Greeks and Romans.

Soon the Italian cities became centers of the "new learning," as it was called. Scholars collected every ancient work they could lay their hands on and had copies of it made. They ransacked monasteries and cathedrals and searched every out-of-the-way place, bringing to light many long-forgotten manuscripts. They read the poems of Homer and Virgil, the stately orations of Cicero, and other Greek and Roman authors.

The interest in the new learning spread all over Europe. Professors at the universities began teaching the Greek and Latin languages and reading the literature to the young men they taught. Thus what was known as the classical course of study was introduced into the universities and came to be regarded as the most important part of the education of a cultured gentleman. It has held this place until very recently in our colleges and universities.

The growth of trade in the latter part of the Middle Ages also contributed to the spread of education. Merchants and their clerks found that they needed to know how to read, write, and keep accounts in order to carry on their business. So rich merchants founded trade schools, where instruction was given in reading and writing and arithmetic to help boys who wanted to go into business.

Trade made quicker methods of reckoning necessary. Ever since Roman times the people of Europe had been using the old clumsy Roman symbols—I, II, III, IV, V, X, L, C, and so on. Computing with the Roman numerals was a very complicated process. It is very difficult to divide XLVIII by VIII, although it is quite easy to divide 48 by 8. The difficulty of calculating with the Roman numerals made it impossible to calculate merely by writing numbers as we do today. It was necessary to use counting boards and other devices. From the East came the Arabic numerals, which made bookkeeping much simpler. When the new system of numerals first became known there was much prejudice against them, as they were thought to be a heathen invention and not proper for use in Christian countries. However, when people discovered that they were a great labor-saving device their use spread rapidly.

It is hard to think of anything that had a greater influence on the spread of education than printing. The invention of printing made it easy to spread knowledge abroad in every land. As books became cheaper even people of small means could afford to buy them. Many people therefore learned to read to find out what was in the new books. Thus through the printing press knowledge which for so many centuries had been enjoyed only by the monks and a few other people was put within the reach of everyone. More and more people learned to read; thus printing was one of the important means of bringing to an end the widespread ignorance and superstition of the Middle Ages.

The Bible also helped to educate people. Thousands of humble folk learned to read in order that they might study the Scriptures for themselves. Schools were founded to teach children to read the Bible and to instruct them in religion. Thus the ability to read became more widespread than ever.

XXVII

Modern Literatures Begin

WITH so much happening to stir their thoughts and imaginations men began writing to express the ideas teeming in their minds. In almost every country people began writing histories, books of travel stories, poems, plays.

Throughout most of the Middle Ages Latin was the language of the men of culture throughout Europe, and all books were written in Latin. But during those ages each country was developing a language of its own. France and the southern countries, Italy, Spain, and Portugal, were developing languages derived from the Latin. Those of the northern countries grew from the languages which the original tribes had spoken. From the various languages used by the German barbarians, German, English, Swedish, Norwegian, and Danish were developed.

The earliest language in England was Anglo-Saxon. The Normans introduced Norman French, and for about three hundred years after the Norman Conquest there were two languages in England. The Normans used French, and this was the language of the court and the aristocracy. The lower classes still clung to their mother tongue,-Anglo-Saxon. During the centuries when the Anglo-Saxons and the Normans were forming a nation the two languages gradually grew into the English language.

In the later Middle Ages men began writing in the language of their own people. We have seen that Chaucer, the great English poet of the fourteenth century, wrote his *Canterbury Tales* in English. Other writers in other countries began doing the same. Dante, Petrarch, and Boccaccio, Italian poets, wrote their poems in Italian. By the fourteenth or fifteenth centuries every nation came to have a literature of its own. This literature dealt not with heroes, or saints and martyrs, as did most of the medieval literature, but with the life of the day.

In England this new era of literature found its highest expression in the latter part of the fifteenth century in the reign of Queen Elizabeth. By that time England had become a great power, and the people were filled with a great patriotic pride. Full of joy and interest in life and delight in nature, men found it easy to give vent to their thoughts and feelings in beautiful language. Someone has said that England at this time was "a nest of singing birds," for it seemed as if everyone was writing poetry. Sir Walter Raleigh and Sir Philip Sidney wrote poems. Ben Jonson wrote the lovely little lyric beginning:

> *Drink to me only with thine eyes,*
> *And I will pledge with mine;*
> *Or leave a kiss but in the cup*
> *And I'll not look for wine.*

And Christopher Marlowe this one:

Come live with me and be my love,
And we will all the pleasures prove
That hills and valleys, dales and fields,
Or woods or steepy mountain yields.

And we will sit upon the rocks,
And see the shepherds feed their flocks
By shallow rivers, to whose falls
Melodious birds sing madrigals.

And I will make thee beds of roses,
And a thousand fragrant posies;
A cap of flowers, and a kirtle
Embroider'd all with leaves of myrtle.

A gown made of the finest wool,
Which from our pretty lambs we pull;
Fair-lined slippers for the cold,
With buckles of the purest gold.

A belt of straw and ivy buds,
With coral clasps and amber studs:
And if these pleasures may thee move
Come live with me and be my love.

The shepherd swains shall dance and sing
For thy delight each May morning:

If these delights thy mind may move,
Then live with me and be my love.

Shakespeare wrote many lyrics in his plays. One of the finest
is

> *Hark! hark! the lark at heaven's gate sings,*
> *And Phoebus 'gins arise,*
> *His steeds to water at those springs*
> *Of chaliced flowers that lies;*
> *And winking Mary-buds begin*
> *To ope their golden eyes:*
> *With everything that pretty bin,*
> *My lady sweet, arise!*
> *Arise, arise!*

There were many, many others. They were gay, light-
hearted little poems, full of love and beauty and joy in life,
in keeping with the youthful spirit of the time.

This age found its greatest expression in the drama. The
old mystery and miracle plays were still sometimes acted
by companies of tradesmen. But men began writing plays
in which the characters were not taken from the Bible but
were like real men and women who acted and felt as real
people would feel and act under various circumstances. As
the taste for plays grew, bands of players strolled about the
country acting in towns and villages. There were no theaters;
the courtyards of the inns served as playhouses.

By the time of Elizabeth the acting of plays had become
268

so popular that theaters were built and regular companies of players were formed. The theaters were usually round or

A theater of Shakespeare's time. (From an old print.)

octagonal in shape. The cheapest part of the theater was the floor in front of the stage—called the pit—which was

269

left entirely open to the sky and spectators stood to witness the play just as they had done in the inn yards. The rich who could afford to pay more had seats on the stage or in little boxes and galleries around the walls. Sometimes those sitting on the stage made remarks to the actors, telling them

William Shakespeare. (From the first edition of his plays.)

what they thought of their playing, and if the "groundlings," as the people in the pit were called, did not like a play they would groan, howl, mew like cats, or perhaps hiss the actors off the stage.

Little attention was paid to scenery or stage properties. Much was left to the imagination of the audience. The stage was merely a platform, and a sign would tell the audience where the scene was meant to be played. When the scene was supposed to be changed a new sign was hung up.

In some such simple fashion as this plays were presented to Elizabethan audiences.

Among the greatest dramatists of that day was William Shakespeare. He understood human nature and appreciated the thoughts and feelings of all sorts of people. Though the characters of his plays have the flavor of his time they are so true to life that we still enjoy his plays today even although more than three hundred years have passed since they were written. They loved and suffered, had their joys and sorrows, and thought and did things that anyone might think and say and do in similar circumstances. Shakespeare was the greatest writer of plays the world has ever known, and his plays are still acted in almost every country of the world.

XXVIII

Great Artists

WHILE literature and learning were being revived, art received a fresh inspiration, and in the latter part of the fifteenth century and the first half of the sixteenth century came some of the greatest artists the world has ever known.

Of all the towns of Europe during the Renaissance none was more beautiful than Florence in the northern part of Italy. The people of Florence loved beauty so much that they wanted it all about them, so Florence became a great center of art. Sculptors and painters and other artists helped to make their city one of the most splendid in the world at that time. They built beautiful buildings and covered the walls with paintings. They adorned the walls of their churches with marvelous pictures. They constructed palaces with plaques of terra cotta set in their walls, and courtyards with fountains and lovely statues. Some of the greatest painters the world has ever known lived in Florence or did their best work there during the later Middle Ages.

One of the earliest artists of Florence was Giotto di Bondone, usually known as Giotto. When he was a little boy he took care of his father's sheep in the country. The story goes that the noted painter Cimabue, happening to go into the country one day, came upon a bronzed shepherd boy in charge of a flock of sheep. While he watched his sheep he drew pictures of them with a sharp-pointed stone on the smooth surface of a rock. Cimabue was so struck with the boy's talent that he took him to his home and taught him. In time the boy surpassed his master and became the wonder of his age.

Not only did Giotto adorn Florence with pictures, he carved and worked in marble as well. As the result of his work a beautiful bell tower rose near the cathedral, slender and graceful, from which the bells pealed calling the people to church. In those days artists were thought of as fine craftsmen. Each had a little shop where he and the apprentices, who were learning art under the master, worked. Assisted by his pupils Giotto carved exquisite figures on the bell tower. Giotto not only beautified Florence, but he worked in other towns of Italy. On the walls of the church at Assisi he painted scenes from the life of the good St. Francis.

In the center of Florence was the baptistry of St. John, a little eight-sided church where every baby born in Florence was brought to be baptized. For it the sculptor Lorenzo Ghiberti spent more than twenty years making bronze doors. Ten scenes from the Bible, surrounded by exquisite borders of foliage, fruits, birds, and animals, he made to decorate each door.

Luca della Robbia, who had studied with Ghiberti, designed and carved a choir gallery for the cathedral of his beloved Florence and made panels illustrating the hundred and fiftieth psalm:

Praise ye the Lord.

*Praise Him with the sound of the trumpet; praise Him with
the psaltery and the harp.*

*Praise Him with the timbrel and dance; praise Him with
stringed instruments and organs.*

*Praise Him upon the loud cymbals; praise him upon the
high sounding cymbals.*

Let everything that hath breath praise the Lord.

In ten lovely panels della Robbia carved happy children,
singing, playing trumpets, beating drums and tambourines,
or making music on lutes and lyres. Their expressions are so
natural that they seem like real children.

In the fifteenth century the Medici, a family of merchants
in Florence, rose to great wealth. The Medicis loved beautiful things and devoted much of their money to making
Florence beautiful. The most famous member of this family
was Lorenzo de Medici, often called Lorenzo the Magnificent. Lorenzo gathered about him the young artists of his
day. He appointed a noted sculptor to give lessons to all
who would profit by instruction.

To Lorenzo's school came a youth named Michelangelo.
Lorenzo soon recognized the genius of the young sculptor.
He took him to his palace and treated him as one of his own
children. Soon Michelangelo was able to do a piece of work
which made him famous throughout Italy. There lay in
Florence a huge block of marble that an earlier sculptor had
begun work on and had left unfinished. Michelangelo
begged permission to use it. This was given, and he set to

274

The Singing Boys, one of the panels made by Luca della Robbia for the cathedral in Florence.

work. For three years he toiled at a piece of sculpture. Then, when he had finished it, he summoned his friends to see a gigantic statue of David as a youth ready to slay the giant Goliath. Everyone recognized the greatness of his work.

For the tomb of one of the popes Michelangelo carved a statue of Moses. If you look at the picture on the page opposite you will see that he has horns on his head. The Bible says that the face of Moses shone with light when he came down from Mt. Sinai. In early translations of the Bible the rays of light were called by the translator horns, and it is for that reason that Michelangelo carved Moses with horns.

Many of the artists of the Renaissance practiced more than one art. Michelangelo proved to be as much a master with his paintbrush as with his chisel. The best artists of Italy were summoned to Rome by the Pope to decorate the Vatican, the palace of the Popes, which was then being built. The Pope called Michelangelo to paint pictures on the ceiling of the Sistine Chapel.

As the ceiling of the chapel was curved Michelangelo had to do much of his painting lying flat on his back on a high scaffolding. "So weary I get lying on my back, looking upward," he said, "pains shoot through my head, my neck, my eyes. In truth I am getting so that I cannot read except when I am lying upon my back and holding my paper over my head."

It took Michelangelo four years to finish the frescoes in the chapel. They are a series of scenes from the Bible representing the creation, the birth of man, and so on. These still

276

Moses, by Michelangelo.

remain today among the most wonderful paintings in the world.

Another artist of the time was Leonardo da Vinci, a many-sided genius. He was a scientist, an engineer, an architect, a sculptor, a poet, as well as a great artist. Many of his pictures have been destroyed, but we still have two of his finest. One of these is the "Last Supper," which he painted on the wall of a monastery in Milan. It is said that he often worked on it from sunrise to dark, forgetful of both eating and drinking, but painting without ceasing. The picture shows Christ and his twelve disciples seated at a long table. Christ has just said to the apostles: "One of you will betray me," and Leonardo shows by the gestures and the expressions on the faces of the apostles how they felt when they heard these terrible words. Another of Leonardo's great paintings is of the beautiful Mona Lisa, a Florentine lady whose haunting smile delighted him. He spent four years working on it.

Many of the Italian artists, steeped in the medieval spirit, painted only religious subjects. They loved to paint the madonna clad in azure, the color of heaven, with her child, and surrounded by adoring angels, or with dusky-visaged kings kneeling to offer their gifts of frankincense and myrrh. The painter Raphael painted many pictures, but he is best remembered for his lovely madonnas. His masterpiece is the Sistine Madonna, named from the church where it first hung.

The artists of the later Middle Ages began appreciating the beauty of this world and life and showing them in their

278

Mona Lisa, by Leonardo da Vinci.

paintings. An artist named Alessandro Botticelli was among the first to paint pictures of things that were not in the Bible. He loved especially to paint pictures of Greek gods and goddesses. Two of his best-known pictures are the "Birth of Venus" and the lovely allegory, "Spring," with Venus, Cupid, and the Three Graces. The true spirit of beauty dwelt within him, and all that he painted was graceful in form and beautiful in color.

Another important center of artistic activity in the sixteenth century was Venice. The distinguishing characteristic of the Venetian painters is their glowing colors. This was strikingly exemplified in the paintings of Titian, the most famous of the Venetian painters.

Artists from the northern countries were attracted to Italy by the renown of the Italian masters and, after learning all that Italy could teach them, returned to practice their art in their own countries; but their paintings had not the grace and charm of the Italian artists. The first of the famous Flemish artists were two brothers by the name of Van Eyck, who worked in Bruges. Painters also appeared in Germany. Albrecht Dürer and Hans Holbein were the greatest German artists of this time. Dürer is most famous for his wonderful woodcuts and engravings, which have perhaps never been excelled.

These are just a few of the many artists who lived and worked during the great period of the Renaissance. The pictures painted by these and others are today the priceless treasures of art galleries and churches of Europe, and some of them are in art museums of this country.

XXIX

From Magic to Science

THE greater part of the Middle Ages was a time of wide-spread ignorance and superstition. Many of our fairy tales have come down to us from the time when most people really believed in supernatural beings. It was an imaginative age, and men fancied that there were all sorts of strange creatures in existence—hobgoblins, pixies, trolls, and so on. Fiends and monsters inhabited lonely marshes, giants lived in the forests, evil spirits haunted solitary places, and ghosts stalked over the land by night. Witches were people who were supposed to be in league with the devil. They had the power to change themselves into animals, to make themselves invisible, to creep through keyholes. At night they rode through the air on broomsticks and by their diabolical arts could bring much misfortune upon their victims. This belief led to much persecution during the Middle Ages, and many harmless old women, accused of being witches, were tortured or put to death.

The people of the Middle Ages knew little about nature. Various plants were thought to have remarkable powers, according to the shape of their leaves or petals. Wood sorrel, being shaped like a heart, was supposed to be a remedy for

281

heart ailments; liverwort, resembling the form of the liver, was for liver complaints. There were books describing all kinds of fabulous beasts and giving astonishing habits to real animals. Everyone believed in strange creatures, like the dragon and the phoenix, a bird which after it had lived for five hundred years burned itself to death and then rose full-grown from its own ashes. Another fabulous animal was the unicorn, which had the body of a horse, the beard of a goat, and a long, sharp horn in the middle of its forehead.

Magicians of all sorts flourished. They professed to reveal the future, and they made charms and lucky pieces, which were worn by people to keep away bad luck or illness, and powders, which, mixed with food or drink, were thought to inspire hatred or love in the one consuming them.

Medieval people believed that the lives of men were controlled by the influence of the stars. A man who could interpret the significance of the heavens was called an astrologer. It was thought that each man's life was shaped by the movements of certain stars in a wide belt around the heavens called the zodiac. There were twelve constellations, one for each month. The constellation that was in the heavens above the horizon at the time of a child's birth was supposed to influence his nature and fate in life. By knowing it, a person would learn what he could do to be successful. At certain times the stars were supposed to be favorable to certain undertakings, and at other times unfavorable. People consulted astrologers about the proper time to begin a journey or a business undertaking, about a favorable day for a marriage or the coronation of a king.

From Magic to Science

There were other men, called alchemists, who tried to pry into the secrets of nature. They were seeking to discover what was called the philosopher's stone. This magic substance, it was thought, could be dissolved and the liquid made from it would turn any common metal, like copper or

An alchemist's laboratory. (From a painting by David Teniers.)

iron, into gold. A tiny drop of it taken as medicine would prolong life indefinitely and convert tottering old age into youth and beauty. Secretly the alchemists worked in dark underground laboratories cluttered up with furnaces, bellows, crucibles, and odd-shaped bottles filled with queer

283

medicines. They ground powders, burned various substances making weird and mysterious lights, and mixed fluids, watching the changes that took place in them. They distilled and redistilled liquids, always hoping to make the long-sought discovery.

For centuries the alchemists pursued their search for the philosopher's stone. They never found it, but in their experiments they stumbled upon much useful knowledge about various substances, which were of value to later scientists, and without knowing it they laid the foundation for our modern science of chemistry.

Such fanciful ideas about nature seem absurd to us today, but medieval people believed them implicitly. The most improbable things were repeated from generation to generation without its ever occurring to anyone to inquire whether there was any truth in them, but as men came to know more about nature they were gradually dispelled.

During the Middle Ages learned men spent much of their time studying what the ancient thinkers, especially Aristotle, believed about the world and reasoned little themselves about what the authorities taught, never questioning any facts stated by them. As long as men depended entirely on what other men said and made no attempt to prove the truth of their theories progress in science was impossible. But a new spirit was coming to men, and a few leading thinkers were beginning to see that many theories which had been accepted for centuries were not true. As early as the thirteenth century there were a few men who criticized the custom of relying upon Aristotle for all knowledge. The most famous of these was an English scientist, Roger Bacon, a Franciscan monk and a highly educated scholar.

At a time when Aristotle's influence was unbounded Roger Bacon turned away from it, believing that scholars should search for the truth themselves by observation and

Roger Bacon. (From a fifteenth-century manuscript in the Bodleian Library at Oxford.)

experiment. Ignorance, he said, was caused because people had too much respect for authority and custom and were too ready to believe things just because other people believed them. "If I had my way," he wrote, "I would burn all the books of Aristotle, for the study of them can only lead to a loss of time, produce error, and increase intolerance."

285

Not content, then, with merely learning from books, Roger Bacon devoted himself to making experiments and trying to learn some of the secrets of nature. He spent years in patient search for the truth. He set up a laboratory and it is said that people going by used to peep in at him at work and then run away in terror, declaring to their neighbors that they saw the devil with hoofs and horns, spouting fire, working there. In the course of his experiments Roger Bacon seems to have worked out a simple steam engine, and perhaps it was this engine, with its fire and steam, which the people mistook for the devil. He also experimented with a mixture of saltpeter, charcoal, and sulphur. One day this mixture exploded, and people believed more than ever that Roger Bacon was in league with the evil one.

As news of his activities spread Bacon came to be looked upon as a wizard with strange magic powers. In those days it was dangerous for a person to know too much, and Roger Bacon was put in prison, where he remained for a number of years.

Roger Bacon was a thinker far ahead of his time. How interesting it is to know that away back in the thirteenth century he prophesied things which only in modern times have come true! In one of his writings he says:

Instruments for navigation can be made which will do away with the necessity of rowers, so that great ships in rivers and on the sea shall be borne about with greater speed than if they were full of rowers. Likewise carriages can be constructed so that without animals to draw them they may be moved with incredible speed. Machines for flying can be made in which a man may sit in the middle turning some device by which artificial wings are made to strike the air in the manner of a flying bird.

Thus seven hundred years ago Roger Bacon foretold the steamship, the locomotive, and the airplane.

For several centuries after Roger Bacon, who died in 1294, there was little advance in science. Then in the sixteenth and seventeenth centuries came two great original thinkers who laid the foundation of modern astronomy.

The great astronomer of the ancient Greeks was Claudius Ptolemy, who lived in Alexandria in the second century after Christ. Ptolemy believed that the earth was the center of the universe and that the sun, moon, and stars revolved around it. All during the Middle Ages the ideas of Ptolemy were accepted without question. But toward the end of the fifteenth century came a man named Nicolas Copernicus whose ideas were to make a profound change in people's thinking about the earth.

Nicolas Copernicus was born in Poland in 1473. He went to the best schools of his day and afterward to the University of Cracow, where he studied mathematics and astronomy under learned professors. From his earliest childhood he had always had a great interest in the heavens. Often he sat up all night watching the stars from the high steeple of the cathedral of his town. He had no telescope to aid him, because it had not yet been invented, but he noted carefully the travels of the stars. He recorded his observations and compiled tables showing their motions. While he was observing

287

the stars he read carefully the explanation that Ptolemy and other astronomers had given of the movement of the sun and the stars, but he could not make them agree with what he himself observed. At last, after years of patient study, he came to the conclusion that the earth and the other planets revolved about the sun.

In 1507 he began writing a book called *De Revolutionibus Orbium Coelestium* (a long title in Latin which means, *Concerning the Revolutions of the Heavenly Bodies*) in which he gave his reasons for thinking that Ptolemy was mistaken in his theory. For years he kept his manuscript without having it printed, for he knew what great offense such new ideas would give. But in 1541, when he was nearly seventy years old, he allowed it to be printed. The first copy of it reached him just before he died.

It was not until the next century that the theory of Copernicus was confirmed, by an Italian scientist, Galileo.

Among the eager young men who were flocking to the universities of Europe was Galileo Galilei, a youth of Pisa, who entered the university of his native town. Later he lectured in the University of Padua. He gave a great deal of his time to the study of astronomy and soon became convinced that the theory of Copernicus was true. But it was difficult to prove this new belief. Then, in 1609, occurred an event which made this possible.

One day Galileo heard that Hans Lippershey, a Dutch spectacle maker, had made a curious instrument which made distant objects appear close at hand and much larger than they did when viewed by the eye alone. The story is

288

told that the children of the spectacle maker were playing one day with two powerful magnifying glasses and happened to place one behind the other in such a position that the weather cock on the church steeple seemed to be very near. The father, when he learned about this, fixed the glasses in a tube and made rough spyglasses as toys.

When Galileo heard of these magic glasses he saw at once what a valuable help they would be in studying the distant stars. He decided to try to make one himself. Into one end of a lead pipe he fastened a convex glass and in the other a concave glass. To his delight he found that this simple device made objects appear several times as large as when looked at with the eye unaided.

Night after night Galileo ascended a high tower and pointed his little telescope toward the heavens, and mystery after mystery of the night sky was unfolded to his wondering gaze.

For centuries people had known that certain stars change their position through the year. The Greeks called these stars planets, which means wanderers. Jupiter was a planet, which, because of its great size and brilliant light, was always an object of great interest to men who studied the stars. One evening, in 1609, Galileo turned his telescope on Jupiter and made a startling discovery. There were four tiny stars close by which could not be seen without a telescope. Two of them were on the east side and two on the west side. Galileo waited eagerly for the next night to look at them again. That night the two stars which had been on the east side had moved around to the west. Galileo was quite puzzled by this and watched and watched for many nights, whenever the clouds would allow him to see the stars. At last, after observing them many times, he came to the conclusion that they were circling around Jupiter.

Galileo.

Galileo subjected all the planets to his scrutinizing gaze. One discovery followed another, and there never ceased to be a new marvel to look at. No longer was there any doubt in his mind that the wandering planets, of which our earth is one, traveled about the sun.

The news of Galileo's discoveries soon spread and startled the world. Many people were alarmed at the thought that our earth was not the center of the universe, as had been believed for so many centuries. It was thought wicked to hold such beliefs. Galileo was warned to be silent. But he went on with his observations undisturbed by this opposition and constantly announced new wonders.

Devout churchmen thought that this new theory contradicted statements in the Bible, which made the earth the center of God's creation. Galileo was summoned to Rome to explain his views and threatened with punishment unless he would "abandon and cease to teach his false, impious, and heretical opinions." But, unwearying in his effort to place science upon a reasonable basis, he continued his study and in 1632 he wrote a book called *The System of the World of Galileo Galilei* in which he clearly stated his views and his reasons for rejecting the old theories about the earth and accepting the new. The judges of the Inquisition summoned Galileo to appear before them. By that time Galileo was an old man seventy years of age. Completely broken by the terrible ordeal the venerable scientist said: "I am in your hands. Do with me as you will." He was made to swear that it was not true that the earth moves about the sun and that he would never again in words or in writing spread this heresy. It seems very sad that Galileo should have been forced to do this.

In 1642 Galileo died, having established the truth of the theory of Copernicus, which is the basis of our modern science of astronomy.

Other scientists were working in the field of physics and in other sciences. Scientific thinkers who came later built upon the work of these pioneers in science at the end of the Middle Ages and thus laid the foundation for the age of modern science, in which we are living today.

XXX

Nations Grow Strong

TODAY we are so accustomed to the idea of belonging to some particular nation it is hard to realize that in medieval times people thought of themselves not so much as English, French, or some other nationality, but as the vassals of some noble. To the mass of the people the king meant little. They were loyal not to their king but to their feudal lords.

Every castle with its surrounding land was like a little independent kingdom ruled over by its lord, and his power was absolute. Every dweller within his domain was subject to his authority. He had hundreds of bold men who had sworn to fight for him, and on his vast estates he had multitudes of serfs laboring to support him and his fighting men. He made the laws for his territory. He went to war whenever he pleased without asking the consent of the king. All through the Middle Ages there was a more or less constant struggle between the kings and the nobles in the various countries. Often the kings were surpassed in power by their own nobles. Often a feudal lord had more land, more vassals, and more men at arms than his king had. Often a noble waged war on another in spite of anything the king could do. The victor would seize the land of his enemy and add it to his own possessions. Sometimes a noble, more powerful than his king, rose in arms against him, calling upon his vassals to follow him, and they had to obey. Thus the nobles were able to do pretty much as they pleased, and disorder and lawlessness prevailed in many countries.

But there were many influences at work which gradually weakened the power of the nobles and strengthened that of the kings. The Crusades did much to undermine the power of the nobles. Hundreds of thousands of Crusaders were ruined by pledging their lands to raise money for their expeditions to the East. Many of them never returned from the Holy Land, and their estates were taken by the kings. Many more were killed in the wars which they ceaselessly waged with one another. Finally came the introduction of gunpowder, and the changes which it brought about in warfare brought to an end the supremacy of the feudal lords.

No one knows just when or by whom gunpowder was invented, but it was used to make fireworks and rockets in China long before it was known in Europe. In the fourteenth century the Moors introduced it into Europe. As long as the bow and arrow, the sword, and the lance were the chief weapons of war the feudal lords, intrenched in their massive castles or mounted on horses and covered with heavy steel armor, were invincible. But when cannon came to replace medieval siege weapons, and guns and bullets took the place of spears and the crossbow, the usefulness of the castle fortress and armor came to an end, for cannon could shatter the most solid masonry, and no armor was proof against a bullet.

294

The towns also helped to increase the power of kings. The kings often favored the townspeople in their struggles with the nobles and, on the other hand, were glad to have the help of the towns. They needed money to carry on the work of government, and the wealthy townsmen were willing to supply it if the kings would give them protection. The people of the towns, engaged largely in trade, came to see that it was better for them to have a central authority strong enough to curb the lawless nobles. Wise kings realized that promoting the welfare of the majority of their people was to their advantage. If the people were prosperous the government could get more money. Laws were therefore enacted to promote the general welfare.

With the money the kings received from the towns they were able to employ professional soldiers, and their armies of trained troops, supplied with guns and cannon, battered down castle walls and overthrew one great lord after another, taking possession of their territory. Thus it was gradually around the king that each country grew into a nation.

As the kings became stronger people came to think less and less about whose vassals they were and more and more about their country with the king as the head. Thus the kings welded all classes of people into a nation under the same government, and each country developed a distinctively national life, with its own interests. The people of each nation spoke the same language; they had uniform laws and the same customs. The spread of printed books enabled people to know more about their country, and national literatures grew up. Writers related the proud facts

295

of each nation's historic past, poets sang of national heroes, national anthems were sung by the people, and every nation had its flag which was its national symbol. All these things strengthened the bonds of the people within each country. They became conscious of being part of a great nation with a feeling of pride in it and devotion to it which we call patriotism.

By the sixteenth century the governments of many of the countries of western Europe came to be in the hands of strong monarchs, but this was especially true in France, England, and Spain. Until the year 1479 Spain was divided into little kingdoms, the most important of which were held by the Moors. By the marriage of Ferdinand of Aragon and Isabella of Castile in 1479 these two kingdoms were united. They employed their combined strength against the Moors, who were forced to surrender to them, and then Spain came under their rule. United and peaceful at home, Spain became strong and prosperous and advanced to a foremost place in European affairs.

In England, in the sixteenth century, a powerful family of rulers, called the Tudors, came to the throne. They had crushed feudalism, and the power which had formerly been divided among the nobles was now concentrated in their hands. Though the Tudors were despotic they were excellent rulers and gave England order and prosperity. They were therefore popular with the middle class. During their reigns Parliament was ever ready to carry out their wishes.

In Germany and Italy no ruler became strong enough to unite the whole country under one government, but for a long time after the Middle Ages they were made up of separate states which were often at war with one another.

In the struggle between the kings and the nobles the kings, through the help of the middle-class merchants, had won out. Some of the kings tried to become absolute monarchs, and then the people found that they were merely exchanging the despotism of the feudal barons for the despotism of kings. In later centuries the kings were in almost constant conflict with the middle class. In this long struggle the men who had grown rich through industry and trade came to exert an ever-increasing influence upon European affairs and in time were to wage a successful struggle against the tyrannical rule of kings. In England during the time of the Stuart kings, who followed the Tudors on the throne, Parliament, through the influence of the middle class, dethroned two kings and finally set on the throne the person they chose to rule over them.

XXXI

The Boundaries of the Known World Widen

Most of the people of the Middle Ages knew little about the world in which they lived. There was not much travel-

Strange people, half man and half beast, were believed to dwell in faraway parts of the world. Here is a picture of a man-dog, man-bull, man-wolf, and man-pig from a medieval book describing the marvels of the world.

ing, and people for the most part knew only their own communities. The superstitious minds of the day peopled remote regions of the world with all sorts of wonders and terrors.

Unknown lands were thought to be inhabited by strange beasts and monstrous folk, some one-eyed, some headless, some with the heads of different kinds of animals.

The Crusades first gave the people of Europe knowledge of distant lands. For two hundred years the Crusaders flocked to the East and saw strange countries and strange people. Their tales on their return stimulated the interest of other people and led to greater travel. Traders and missionaries also went to the East, and Marco Polo's account of the wonders of Cathay led to increased interest in faraway places. In this way the boundaries of the known world gradually began to widen. But, even so, people had no idea of the true size and shape of the earth.

Greek scholars had written numerous books on geography, and Claudius Ptolemy, the Greek astronomer, was also a geographer. He wrote a geography and drew maps which gave a very accurate idea of the world as it was known in his day. But Ptolemy's work was forgotten or neglected for more than a thousand years.

All through the Middle Ages geographers made maps of the world, but as they knew very little about the real world, they filled in from their imaginations the places they did not know about and populated unknown regions with strange beasts and people. They also mingled their ideas of religion with their ideas of geography. They read in the Bible: "Thus saith the Lord God: This is Jerusalem. I have set it in the midst of the nations and countries that are round about it," and they therefore placed Jerusalem in the center of the world. A reference in Isaiah to "the four corners of the earth" led them to believe that the earth was rectangular in shape, and they therefore made it so.

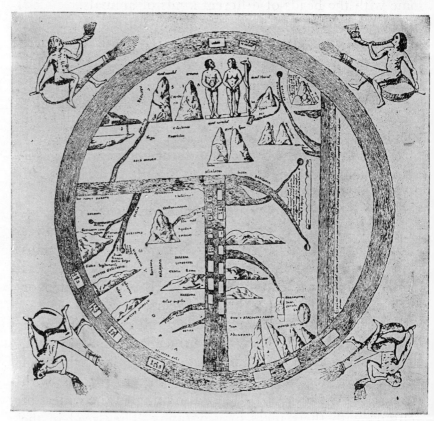

The Turin Map of the World.

One of the earliest maps that has come down to us is that made by a monk named Cosmas. The earth is rectangular and surrounded by the ocean. Beyond this ocean is Paradise,

300

An Anglo-Saxon map of the world, made in the tenth century.

described by Cosmas as "the earth beyond the ocean where men dwelt before the flood." Four deep gulfs penetrate the earth from the ocean, and the rivers which flowed from Paradise are also shown. In medallions are figures blowing trumpets, representing the four winds of the world. Another quaint representation of the earth is the Turin Map. The world is divided into three parts—Europe, Asia, and Africa. Adam and Eve stand at the top with the serpent, and the mountains and rivers and the four winds of heaven are shown.

Another famous medieval map is the Anglo-Saxon map of the world made in the tenth century. A map of the thirteenth century still preserved in Hereford Cathedral in England is among the most interesting of the medieval maps. These maps are of interest to us today because they show how little the people of the Middle Ages knew about the real world.

For centuries most of men's voyaging had been on the Mediterranean Sea. This great land-locked body of water was fairly calm, and its many inlets and bays offered safe harbors for ships. Few ships were to be seen on the Atlantic Ocean except near the sheltering coasts. Seamen had no instruments to guide them when they were far out of sight of land. They had no way of steering their ships except by the sun in the daytime and the North Star by night. In times of storm or fog, or on nights when there were no stars to be seen, a ship might be hopelessly lost on the sea.

Added to these real dangers of ocean voyaging were the superstitious fears of the day. The sea, so full of strange

Monsters of the sea of darkness as imagined by a sixteenth-century artist. (From the *Cosmographiae Universalis* by Sebastian Münster.)

creatures, stirred the imagination of sailors. Terrifying legends had grown up about the Sea of Darkness, as the Atlantic Ocean was called. The unknown deep was supposed to be haunted by horrible monsters and sea serpents that would drag ships down and strangle all on board. It was said that at the equator the sun poured down liquid flames into a boiling sea. It is little wonder that mariners refused to venture far out on such dangerous waters. For hundreds of years sailors were content to sail the well-known routes of the Mediterranean. So the Atlantic Ocean stretched away to the west of Europe, a vast unexplored expanse of water. No one knew what lay beyond it. No one dared sail far enough out on it to find out. For centuries the mystery that hung over it hid from the people of Europe knowledge of half the surface of the earth and the two western continents.

In the latter part of the Middle Ages seamen invented some very useful aids for navigating their ships. After the Crusades the compass was introduced into Europe. A compass is a needle which has been magnetized. It always points north. Probably the Chinese were the first to know about it, and then Arab traders in Chinese waters began using it. Through them knowledge of it reached Europe during the Crusades. With its aid sailors could steer their ships over unknown waters even when the sun and stars were not visible.

At first sailors refused to use the compass. They thought there must be some kind of magic in it and were afraid to have anything to do with it. One writer of the time said:

This discovery, so useful to all who travel by sea, must remain concealed until other times because no master mariner dares to use it lest he should fall under the reputation of being a magician, nor would sailors venture themselves out to sea under his command if he took with him an instrument which carries so great an appearance of being constructed under the influence of some infernal spirit.

But gradually sailors came to recognize its usefulness. They found it reliable and a wonderful help in steering their ships. A glance at the compass would tell them where the north was, no matter where they happened to be. So the compass rapidly grew in importance, and by the fourteenth century every Mediterranean ship had one in a little glass-covered box.

But even with the compass mariners could not tell exactly where they were at any particular time. To help them in doing this other instruments came into use. One of them was called the astrolabe. It enabled ship captains to find out how far north or south of the equator they were by measuring the height of the sun over the horizon. This helped them to calculate distance and to steer their ships. When the pitching and rolling of the ship made it difficult to use the astrolabe another instrument, the cross staff, was used, which could be held more steadily in the hands. Holding it up to his eye, with one end pointed to the sun and the other to the horizon, the mariner moved the cross bar on which degrees were marked in such a way as to make it possible to calculate the position of his ship.

There were also great improvements in ships. During the

earlier centuries of the Middle Ages ships were equipped with sails or worked by long oars. Ships that depended on oars were all right for the calm waters of the Mediterranean Sea but could not be used on the rough waters of the ocean. The shipbuilders of the late Middle Ages learned how to build ships propelled by sails alone. Down to the thirteenth century only one mast was used on ships, but in the fourteenth century two and sometimes three masts were used. At first the height of the masts was limited by the size of the trees from which they were made, but later additions in masts were lashed to the tops of these. Sails also showed interesting developments. During the early Middle Ages ships had one square sail which could be used only when the wind was blowing from behind. But sailors learned to manage their sails so that they caught the wind in whatever direction it blew. Each sail was divided into a number of parts, so that one part could be reefed while the rest remained outspread.

Mariners were also aided by a new type of map and chart that came into use in the latter part of the Middle Ages. At that time there grew up the custom among seamen of writing out sailing directions to the places to which they voyaged and selling them to other ship captains. Gradually, instead of writing out the directions, seamen made careful drawings of the coasts along which they sailed. Then other sea captains could buy charts showing the shores of countries as experienced sailors had seen them. Thus mariners were gradually building up maps and charts of the land and sea which were true to fact, and they came to have accurate

306

information about lands they had never seen and how to reach them.

With all these improvements in navigation longer sea voyages were possible, and daring seamen appeared ready to venture beyond the sheltered waters of the Mediterranean on which they had sailed for so many centuries.

XXXII

Across the Sea of Darkness

IT WAS the son of the King of Portugal, Prince Henry, known to history as the Navigator, who first stimulated the people of Europe to go on voyages of exploration that were to make vast changes in the history of the world. For some time Portugal looked with envy upon the rich trade of Venice with the East and longed to have some share in it. Portugal was on the western edge of Europe, fronting the Atlantic Ocean. Her only hope of finding a route to the riches of the East was by the sea. Prince Henry believed that India and the other countries of the East could be reached by sailing around the southern tip of Africa.

Forsaking the court and all the honors it had to offer him, the young prince went to live at one of the dreariest spots on the southern coast of Portugal. There on a bare, rocky headland, washed by the waters of the unexplored Atlantic, he built an observatory and devoted himself to the study of navigation. He gathered around him the best geographers of the day, the most skillful mapmakers, the best shipbuilders of all lands; he built many ships and sought out the most fearless sea captains to sail them. Sailors from all over Europe came to engage in his service.

Across the Sea of Darkness

For many years Portuguese seamen had explored the northwestern coast of Africa and traded with the natives. But at a certain cape they had always turned back. They had named this point of land Cape Non (Cape Not), because they said that the sea beyond it was full of currents "so terrible that no ship having passed the cape would ever be able to return."

Prince Henry tried to teach his captains to pay no attention to such tales, and to pass this seemingly impassable cape and push exploration down the African coast became the purpose of his life. In 1434 Gil Eannes, one of his captains, had orders to sail beyond it. He set out but returned terrified by the tales he had heard. The prince rebuked him for being influenced by such childish ideas. "If there were the slightest authority for such stories," he said, "I would not blame you. But you come to me with tales of seamen who don't know how to use the needle [compass], or sailing charts. Go out again and give no heed to their words, for fame and profit must surely come from your voyage if you but persevere."

With this encouragement Gil Eannes set out once more, and this time the daring captain succeeded in passing the dreaded cape. On his return he reported that he had found the sea beyond it "as easy to sail on as the waters at home."

Fleet after fleet Prince Henry sent down the unknown coast of Africa, and farther and farther south sailed his ships. Little by little the west coast was explored and charted. Sad to say, however, Prince Henry did not live to see his dream of finding the way around Africa to the East realized. But his years of patient work were not in vain, for after his death other Portuguese seamen continued their search. In 1487, a bold captain by the name of Bartholomew Diaz coasted southward, hugging the shore, and reached the cape at the southern tip. Then terrible storms forced him to return to Portugal. Eleven years later another Portuguese seaman, Vasco da Gama, with a fleet of five vessels, rounded the stormy cape and struck northwest over the Indian Ocean, finally reaching the coast of India. The Portuguese had at last found a seaway to the East.

The success of Da Gama brought to an end European trade with the East by the old overland routes that had been followed for so many centuries. The new route enabled Portuguese merchants to sell Eastern goods for much less than the Venetian merchants could sell theirs, because it was cheaper to ship them directly to Europe without all the delay and cost that was necessary in carrying them overland and on the Mediterranean. So the trade of Venice declined, and the days of her greatness as a trading city came to an end. Fleets of Portuguese vessels plied to and fro between the Cape of Good Hope, and Portugal came to be the leading nation in the trade with the East.

While the Portuguese were making their way down the coast of Africa, seeking the East, another seaman, Christopher Columbus, was dreaming of reaching the East by sailing west across the Sea of Darkness. He carefully studied all the best maps of the time. He read Marco Polo's story of Cathay. From the maps the possibility of reaching Asia by a westward route seemed simple enough, for on them there was, of course, no sign of the two Western continents block-

310

Part of the globe made by Martin Behaim in 1492. The large flags show important discoveries made by the Portuguese.

ing the way there. Little dreaming of the immense size of the earth, Columbus thought that such a route to Asia would be much shorter than the one the Portuguese were seeking around Africa.

Columbus could not rest until he had tested out his plan. To make such a trip he needed money and ships. He applied to the King of Portugal for help. But the Portuguese were at that time steadily making their way down the African coast and were confident that they would some day find the route to India. Finally, as you know, he received the necessary help from Spain.

It was hard to get sailors to go on what seemed such a reckless adventure. But, at last, ninety men were found willing to make the voyage. Little did they dream that the whole future history of the world was to be changed by that voyage.

Early in the morning of August 3, 1492, three little ships slipped out of the harbor of Palos and boldly set their course westward over the terrifying Sea of Darkness. As day after day, week after week, passed, and there was nothing but sky and sea to be seen, the sailors became more and more frightened. They thought they would never reach home again, and they tried to make Columbus turn back. But Columbus kept his ships headed westward, and three months after they had left Spain they reached land.

"The gate to the gold and pearls is now open," said Columbus, when he landed, "and precious stones, spices, and a thousand things may surely be expected." He thought that the wild coast did not look much like the coast of Cathay,

312

Columbus bidding farewell to King Ferdinand and Queen Isabella before setting out on the Sea of Darkness. (From De Bry's *America*, published in 1590.)

or India, as described by Marco Polo. There were no splendid cities or jeweled emperors. Perhaps the land was one of the islands Marco Polo had written about. Somewhere among them must be the island of Cipango, with its gold-roofed palaces and rose-colored pearls. When he had found it he would steer for the mainland and deliver the letter which Queen Isabella had given him for the great Khan.

By signs Columbus asked the Indians which way he should go to find Cipango. They told him of a rich island to the south. Columbus sailed in search of it. "For," he tells us, "by the signs the Indians made of its greatness and its gold and pearls, I thought it must be Cipango." But with the most diligent searching Columbus found neither cities nor treasure, and he returned to Spain.

Another voyage, Columbus thought, would surely unlock the Eastern treasure house. He had no difficulty in fitting out a second expedition. On this voyage other islands were discovered, but still the golden East could not be found. Four times Columbus set out and returned without finding India or China. In the meantime Vasco da Gama had found the route to India around Africa. The Portuguese government informed the Spanish king and queen that a nobleman of their court had found the route to the Indies and had brought back "cinnamon, cloves, ginger, nutmeg, pepper, also many stones of all sorts." The fame of Vasco da Gama spread over all Europe. The Spanish people were bitterly disappointed. In the contest between Spain and Portugal for the riches of the East, Portugal had won and Spain had lost.

this narrow, winding strait. His sailors begged him to turn back, but he answered, "If I have to eat the leather of the ship's yards, yet will I go on and do my work."

VICTORIA

Magellan's ship the *Victoria,* the first ship to sail around the world. (From Hulsius' *Collection of Voyages,* published in 1602.)

At last the ships came to the end of the torturous strait, and when Magellan "saw the way open to the other main sea he was so glad thereof that for joy the tears fell from his eyes." The calm waters of the ocean were so pleasant after

317

the terrible storms they had been through that Magellan named the newly found ocean the Pacific, which means peaceful.

Then Magellan boldly struck out northwest on the unknown waters, little dreaming that he had set sail on an ocean which covers nearly half the earth. The days grew to be weeks and the weeks lengthened into months and still there was no land. There was little drinking water, and the food gave out. Many of the crew died of starvation. For more than three months the little fleet struggled westward. At last they reached an island. There in a battle with the natives Magellan and a number of his men were killed.

A single ship, the *Victoria,* all that was left of Magellan's fleet, finally found its way to the Spice Islands, thence across the Indian Ocean, around the Cape of Good Hope, and so back home to Spain. It had sailed around the world.

Magellan's voyage showed that the New World was separated from Asia by a vast ocean, and it proved that the earth was round and that it was much larger than people up to that time had believed.

During the fifteenth and sixteenth centuries the people of Europe learned more about the earth than they had learned in thousands of years before. Shut off from the west by the dreaded Sea of Darkness, for centuries they had been interested in the East. Then, toward the close of the fifteenth century, the ocean to the west was at last ventured upon, and for two hundred years after this intrepid explorers pushed farther and farther into the unknown western
318

world. With each exploration the size of the earth grew until the little medieval world was expanded into a great earth-round world with its masses of land and bodies of water revealed for the first time as they really are.

These great geographical discoveries had a far-reaching effect upon the history of the world. After the discovery of America, trade which for centuries had centered about the Mediterranean Sea, shifted to the Atlantic Ocean, and the nations of Europe facing the Atlantic became the principal trading countries of Europe and the leading nations in her later history.

Our Heritage from the Middle Ages

Conclusion

ALL the great events and discoveries and the splendid achievements of the later centuries of the Middle Ages which we have been describing were signs of a new stage in the intellectual development of the people of Europe. At that time men's minds were stimulated by new ideas and new experiences. Europe was throbbing with new life and new energy. Everywhere men were awakening, eager to study and to learn. They began thinking for themselves. And when they began thinking for themselves they were led to question authority in many fields. Henceforth each individual was to be responsible for his thoughts, his beliefs, his actions.

With this awakening came a new point of view about society. In feudal days the mass of the people were powerless in the hands of a few men who had possession of the land. The people paid in toil and liberty for food, shelter, and safety. But gradually the idea grew among them that the humble man was as important as the man of higher birth, and that every man, however poor or lowly his station, had certain rights. With that idea democracy was born. John Ball, away back in 1381, sounded the note of

323

democracy when he said to the peasants: "Ah, ye good people, things goeth not well in England, nor shall they do, till everything be common, till there be no gentlemen nor villeins, but we be all united together and the lords be no greater masters than we be."

We have followed the struggle of the people of medieval England for better conditions in life, for greater justice, for more freedom. We have seen how through centuries of slow determined progress they won civil and political liberty and secured a government based upon law rather than upon force. In a society protected by the laws which the people themselves made, the lowliest could make his way upward.

The roots of our American civilization lie in the Middle Ages. By the end of the fifteenth century Portugal, Spain, France, and England had well-organized national governments and were ready for new undertakings. The rulers of these countries granted large sums of money to explorers and fitted out ships in quest of new routes to the riches of the East. In the course of these explorations the people of Europe stumbled upon new land in the west and gradually there dawned upon them the realization that undreamed-of wealth existed in this newly found land. Then followed a long struggle among the principal nations of Europe for possession of this land. Thus American history—our own history—begins.

You know from your study of American history how England finally obtained possession of most of the land in America and how the English formed the colonies out of

324

which our nation later grew. These colonists brought with them to their new homes across the sea the ideas, customs, beliefs, and institutions which had developed in Europe during the Middle Ages. American civilization is therefore a continuation of that of medieval Europe.

Most of the people who came to America belonged to the middle and lower classes. Few of the aristocracy came. The people who emigrated to America came with the hope of working out a better, happier life for themselves and their children. It was the hope of greater opportunity in the new country just being opened up which induced many people to leave their homes and friends in the Old World and brave the dangers of life in an unknown, unsettled land. There, far removed from Europe, they believed, they would be able to manage their own affairs. There they would have a better chance to make a living than the Old World offered them. There a man would have the chance to advance as far as his ability could take him.

The English people who settled America were the heirs of the great political traditions of England and they worked out in the New World a political organization similar to that which had been developed in the Mother Country. All the rights and privileges which the people of England had gained at home were granted to the colonists in America. A charter, given by King James to the first colonists who landed at Jamestown, stated:

We do for us, our heirs and successors, declare by these presents, that all and every the persons, being our subjects, which shall dwell and inhabit within every and any of the several colonies and plantations, and every one of their children, which shall happen to be born within any of the limits and precincts of said several colonies and plantations, shall enjoy the liberties, franchises and immunities to all intents and purposes as if they had been abiding and born within this our realm of England.

Not long afterward a plan of government was initiated in Virginia, the first colony, which was "to follow the laws and administration of justice used in the realm of England as near as may be." In time every colony had a government modeled in general upon that of England. Thus the English system of representative government was introduced into this country.

When, after the Revolution, the colonies became an independent nation, they framed a constitution, which was to give to the people of the new nation the freedom won by their forefathers in England. In the Bill of Rights, which is the part of the constitution enumerating the rights of every citizen of the United States, you will find, among others, the following important clauses:

Congress shall make no law respecting an establishment of religion, or prohibiting the free exercise thereof; or abridging the freedom of speech, or of the press; or the right of the people peaceably to assemble, and to petition the government for a redress of grievances.

No person shall . . . be deprived of life, liberty, or property, without due process of law.

In all criminal prosecutions the accused shall enjoy the right to a speedy and public trial, by an impartial jury.

Conclusion

All these rights go back to the days of Magna Charta and to the later struggles of the English people to develop a form of government in which fundamental liberties and social justice should be guaranteed to everyone living under it.

The people of the later Middle Ages were our cultural ancestors. They have bequeathed to us their treasures of art, architecture, and literature. It was at that time, also, that the foundation was laid for much of the scientific knowledge we possess today. The scientists who appeared at the close of the Middle Ages, and who observed and experimented and reasoned on the basis of this observation and experimenting, were the initiators of a long scientific movement which is still going on.

Through the changes that came about in the latter part of the Middle Ages the foundations for a new type of civilization were being laid. Up to that time the people had supplied their wants mainly by agriculture. But with the growth of towns trade and industry developed by leaps and bounds. With the discovery and settling of America commerce took great strides, as European nations gradually realized the riches of the newly opened-up land, which offered new markets for European goods and new materials to take back to Europe. Thus was ushered in a period of tremendous commercial activity. These commercial changes brought about, in later centuries, great changes in the making of goods and thus led to the industrial age in which we are living today.

All that was achieved in the Middle Ages has been

passed on to us. It is indeed a goodly heritage which we have received from those people of far-off medieval days. But much of the work begun by them has not yet been finished. The struggle of the people for better conditions in life is still going on today. In the great forward march of mankind, each age, building on what those who lived here earlier accomplished, has its contribution to make in the never-ending effort of man to make the world a better place for people to live in. We of today must try to play our part intelligently in finding ways of bringing this about.

Index

Index

Index